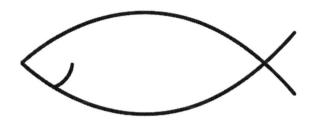

Jesus Makes Salsa by the Seashore

And Other Fresh-Approach
Bible Studies

Troy Dungan

WESTBOW
P R E S S®
A DIVISION OF THOMAS NELSON
& ZONDERVAN

WestBow Press books may be ordered through booksellers or by contacting:

WestBow Press
A Division of Thomas Nelson & Zondervan
1663 Liberty Drive
Bloomington, IN 47403
www.westbowpress.com
1 (866) 928-1240

Because of the dynamic nature of the Internet, any web addresses or links contained in this book may have changed since publication and may no longer be valid. The views expressed in this work are solely those of the author and do not necessarily reflect the views of the publisher, and the publisher hereby disclaims any responsibility for them.

Any people depicted in stock imagery provided by Thinkstock are models, and such images are being used for illustrative purposes only. Certain stock imagery © Thinkstock.

ISBN: 978-1-5127-2642-8 (sc)
ISBN: 978-1-5127-2643-5 (e)

Library of Congress Control Number: 2016900381

Print information available on the last page.

WestBow Press rev. date: 1/26/2016

Jesus Makes Salsa by the Seashore
And Other Fresh Approach Bible Studies
Troy Dungan

FOREWORD

With his inimitable wit, insight, and practical good sense, Troy has put together a collection of studies that will most assuredly enrich the lives of everyone who explores them. And if you can't trust a veteran weatherman, who can you trust? Troy has spent decades divining the hand of God in nature ... and in life.

Dr. Larry Poland
Founding CEO MasterMedia

PREFACE

I became a Christian believer when I was a little kid. Don't ask me about my "Damascus Road Experience." There wasn't one. We lived in a small Texas town where all the people I knew were Christians. At some point, probably when I was seven or eight, I realized that Jesus was the Son of God. He died for my sins. And three days later He rose from the dead that I might have eternal life (and anybody else who believed that).

But I never did much with my Christian belief. Oh, I went to church all my life. I even graduated from Baylor University, a Christian school. But that was about it.

Then, when I was sixty-two years old I had a "chance" meeting with Dr. Larry Poland, CEO of MasterMedia. This is a ministry aimed at the movers and shakers in media and entertainment. I learned that perhaps three-quarters of all media and entertainment in the United States is controlled by fewer than five hundred people, most of them middle-aged to older Jewish men. As Jerry Seinfeld would say, "Not that there's anything wrong with that."

MasterMedia seeks to show these people what their research indicates most evangelical Christians would watch on TV or see in movies. And there are a lot of us. So these industry leaders are interested. The response has been great. Many of these executives have actually become Christian believers. And even those who have not have gained a new respect for and interest in G- and PG-rated entertainment. Although there is still plenty of garbage on TV and movie screens, a lot is going on behind the scenes. One of these things is that MasterMedia has been showing Christian believers in Hollywood and New York that they are not alone.

The first time I heard Larry Poland speak, I learned that there were weekly Bible studies in all the major Hollywood movie studios and also the major TV stations in the Los Angeles area. I was amazed and impressed by that, but not motivated to action. Then I heard Dr. Poland speak twice more in fairly rapid succession. After the third time (as in the old cartoons) a lightbulb came on over my head. I said to myself, "Self, you are supposed to be doing something here."

After considerable prayer and consideration, I found myself walking into the office of the operations manager at WFAA-TV in Dallas to ask if I could have the main conference room at the station for a half hour every Wednesday at 1 p.m. for a Bible study. He paused for a couple of seconds and said, "Well, I guess so. But let me check." He asked the general manager of the station. She asked the corporate legal office. And much to my surprise (and all of theirs too), the answer was yes.

The only caveats were that I did not pressure anyone to attend and that if someone needed the conference room for a business meeting, I would give up the room and find another spot.

The only problem then was that I had never taught a Bible study in my life. How was I going to do this? I found that if you ask the Holy Spirit for help, He gives it to you. I would sit down at my desk at home every Wednesday morning with a pile of source materials, and sure enough I would start to write (in my barely legible longhand) and out would come ... Bible studies. Amazing!

These Bible studies went on for eight years, until a few weeks before I retired from WFAA-TV.

The studies just seemed to work out naturally to about ten minutes. Then I would ask for prayer requests and pray over them. Our group became really tight. Generally we would have about ten people. Sometimes it would be as many as twenty-five. On a few occasions, we would have only three or four. But those turned out to be some of the best days. The people who were supposed to be there were there.

The biggest crowd we ever had was when Dr. Larry Poland "happened to be" in Dallas. We had become close friends by then. It was an honor to have him speak to the group.

The studies in this little book are adaptations of those we did in the conference room at WFAA-TV. When I retired, no one at the station picked up the baton. But the eight years we had there together amounted to a special season in the lives of those of us who shared those Wednesday afternoons. And going through these studies has brought a sweet fragrance of memories. Now it is my privilege to share them with you.

The Bible that I use is:
The Nelson Study Bible
New King James Version
Copyright 1997 by Thomas Nelson Inc.

All Scripture quotes that I use in these Bible studies are taken from this Bible.

Troy Dungan
Dallas, Texas

CHAPTER 1

Jesus Makes Salsa by the Seashore
The Original Fish Tacos

Read John 21.

The setting for this story is the shore of the Sea of Galilee, which is really a lake—Lake Gennesaret—in Israel. This takes place sometime between Jesus's resurrection and His ascension into heaven. Jesus had already appeared to His disciples at least once since being raised from the dead. In John 20, He suddenly appeared in a locked room where His disciples were hiding because they were afraid that the Jewish authorities, after getting rid of Jesus (so they thought), would now be coming after them.

The John 20 appearance was perhaps only twelve hours or so after His resurrection. In verses 19 and 21, He told the disciples to have peace. But they did not quite get it. That was a tall order. They were afraid. But things changed for them big time one verse later in John 20:22, when the Scripture says that He breathed on them and bestowed the Holy Spirit on them. Only then did they really understand fully who Jesus was and what He was teaching them. During their approximately three years of walking with Him, they still only had their human understanding. Now the Holy Spirit illuminated their minds. All the other believers in Israel had to wait until about fifty days later, at the Feast of Pentecost, to receive the filling of the Holy Spirit. As Christians today, we are blessed to receive the filling of the Holy Spirit the moment we believe in Jesus.

So with that background, here in chapter 21, verses 1–14, is the story you have no doubt heard many times. My Bible calls it "Breakfast by the Sea." But there is a really cool twist to the story that you probably have not heard.

Okay, Peter and the guys have been out fishing all night and caught nothing. They were tired and frustrated. Peter saw that someone had built a fire on the beach, but he did not yet realize that it was Jesus. At this point, Jesus, knowing their night's fishing had been unsuccessful, called out to the guys and told them to drop their nets on the other side of the boat. They did so, and suddenly they caught so many fish their nets were strained almost to the point of breaking. Then Jesus told them to bring their fish over to Him.

John then recognized Jesus and told Peter who He was. Peter, always impulsive, jumped over the side of the boat and started swimming toward Jesus. But note what the text here said he did first. Peter put on his outer garment. Normally, one would take off as many clothes as possible before starting to swim. So what's that all about? Peter often made bad decisions. But he had true zeal in his love for Christ. This was no doubt one of those "seemed like a good idea at the time" moments. But thankfully he made it to shore. Meanwhile, the other disciples followed Jesus's instructions and brought the boat with the fish-filled nets to shore near Him.

A point of application for us here is that love for Jesus is manifested in different ways by different believers. We need to let other believers worship Him in their own ways. For instance, some people raise their hands when they sing in church. Some don't. Some kneel to pray. Some don't. We need to cut fellow believers some slack. We don't all have to worship Jesus in exactly the same manner.

So the guys dragged these heavy nets full of fish onto shore near where Jesus had a fire going. The passage then says that He had some fish and bread cooking on the fire. Well, first of all, where do you suppose Jesus got bread, fish, and charcoal early in the morning on a deserted beach? At the 7-11? Nope. We don't know where He got them from. But if anybody could come up with those things in this situation, it would be Jesus—being God and all.

Then He told the disciples to bring Him some of the fish from their catch. If one of the things He already had was fish, why tell them to bring over more fish? What's up with that? If He already had fish cooking, why ask them to bring more? Well, here's the cool twist. The normal Greek word for fish is *ichthus*. (That Christian fish symbol you see on the back of some folks' cars is called an *ichthus*. It means fish. That *ichthus* symbol came to symbolize Jesus). So *ichthus* is the word He used. Bring over some of that *ichthus* that you just caught.

Meanwhile the text uses another word for the "fish" Jesus had on the fire along with the bread. That Greek word is *opsarion*. Now that word *can* mean fish, but it has another meanings as well. It can mean a relish, condiment, or sauce for fish. In context, that is exactly what it means here. Jesus had made salsa to go on the bread He had and the fish the disciples had caught. And the bread would have been unleavened. So right there by the Sea of Galilee that morning, Jesus made the original fish tacos. Would you love to have some of that Jesus salsa? I know I would.

Side note here: Why does the text then say that 153 large fish were in the nets? It is an authenticating detail in the story. And though the nets were stretched beyond their normal strength, they did not break. Our application: our "nets" are as strong as the purpose God has for us.

Now we have had a little fun with this story so far. And by the way, if God does not have a sense of humor, I am in a lot of trouble. But now John 21:15–21 takes a very different and more serious tack.

You will no doubt remember that in the night and early morning of Jesus's illegal trials prior to His crucifixion, Peter denied Him three times. In this passage, Jesus asks Peter three times if he loves Him. Is there a connection? Maybe so. But that is not the point of what is going on here. We need to consider the three Greek words for love. They are *eros, phileo,* and *agapē*. Eros relates to physical love, hence the English word *erotic*. *Phileo* is an affection, sometimes called brotherly love. And *agapē* is unconditional love. God's love for us is *agapē* love.

Now I must add a disclaimer here. Once I taught this study at a church (not my own). Afterward, a retired minister of that church came up and pointed out to me that Jesus and the disciples would have been speaking Aramaic in their conversation. And there is only one word for love in Aramaic. My response was that although that might be true, the New Testament was written in Greek. And two of the Greek words for *love* are used in this passage. I believe that the entire Bible is the divinely inspired Word of God. So I believe the following interpretation is valid.

In verse 15, Jesus asks Peter, "Do you (*agapē*) love Me more than these?" It is commonly taught that "these" meant the other disciples. But the word Jesus used for these was in the neuter. So He would not have meant "Do you love Me more than you love these other guys?" He meant the things of the world, the things that make up everyday life—such as fishing. In any case, Peter answered Jesus, "Lord, You know that I (*phileo*) love You." Wrong answer. Jesus was asking for a commitment of unconditional love from Peter. But to his credit, Peter did not commit to something that he knew at this point he could not give. Jesus then told Peter to feed His lambs.

Lambs need to be fed. Peter was to make sure Jesus's new followers were provided for.

In verse 16, Jesus again asks Peter if he (*agapē*) loves Him. And once again, Peter declines to commit to unconditional love, telling Jesus, "Yes, Lord, You know that I (*phileo*) love You." Jesus told to Peter to tend his sheep—provide spiritual guidance to the followers of Jesus.

Then in verse 17, Jesus asked Peter for a third time if he loved Him. But this time, Jesus used the word *phileo*. The text says that Peter was grieved. Peter said, "Lord, You know all things. You know that I (*phileo*) love You."

Why was Peter grieved? Jesus knew that Peter did not yet have the spiritual strength to commit to *agapē* love. But by changing His word to *phileo* in the third question, Jesus was assuring Peter that He could and would use him as he was. This time, He told Peter to shepherd His sheep, a broader command than feed and tend. Even though Peter was far from perfect, Peter could still serve Christ.

Application for us: Peter was just being honest. And he is an example for us here. Don't tell God you are going to do something you know you won't be able to do. We are also far from perfect. But we can serve Christ.

Later, after an intense forty-eight days or so with the resurrected Christ, Peter was able to come up to *agapē* love for Jesus, fearlessly witnessing for Him. And of course, he eventually suffered a martyr's death for Jesus. *That* was unconditional commitment. *That* was *agapē* love!

But there is one more nugget for us in the last six verses in this chapter. Peter turned and saw John. He said to Jesus, "What about this man?" Jesus said to Peter, "If I will that he remain until I come, what is that to you? You follow Me." Ouch! In other words, mind your own business, Peter. We are not to compare ourselves to others. Just follow Jesus.

And … as good as Pace Picante Sauce is, when I get to heaven, I am really looking forward to some of that Jesus salsa. How about you?

CHAPTER 2

Now *That's* a Fish Story! Featuring Second Chances for the Disobedient

Read the book of Jonah. (It's short.)

Jonah lived in the northern part of Israel in a town called Gath Heper (which was a few miles northeast of Nazareth). He was a prophet, which is what we would call a preacher today. His ministry was in the first half of the eighth century BC. Outside of this book, which bears his name, he is mentioned only one other time in the Old Testament, in 2 Kings 14:25.

But Jonah does get several mentions in the New Testament. And those mentions come from Jesus Himself! In Matthew 12:40–41, Jesus refers to Jonah's three days in the belly of a great fish as an analogy to His own impending death and resurrection three days later. And there are others, about which more later. Now most everybody is at least a little bit familiar with the story of Jonah. But I bet you had to look it up in your Bible's table of contents, didn't you?

Well, in this book God gives Jonah an assignment in the very first sentence of the first chapter: "Now the word of the Lord came to Jonah the son of Amittai, saying, 'Arise, go to Nineveh, that great city and cry out against it; for their wickedness has come up before Me.'"

So the best thing for Jonah to do would have been to get up and follow God's instructions immediately. But, that is *not* what he did. Nineveh, the capital of Assyria, was over five hundred miles from where Jonah lived. And there was no El Al Airline or even Israeli Greyhound Bus service in those days. The way he would have to get to Nineveh would be on foot. And five hundred miles is a long walk.

Even though it was that far away, Jonah had heard of Nineveh. Everybody had. Nineveh's reputation as a city of pride, greed, wickedness, brutality, and adultery was widely known. So, it wasn't so much the great distance that caused Jonah to disobey God. It was that he just did not want the assignment God gave him. It was a test—a trial, a tribulation for him. He flunked the test. He did not want anything to do with such a place. He did not think the Ninevites deserved a warning from God. And he certainly did not want to be the one who delivered it.

So he got up and went all right, but in the opposite direction from Nineveh. He walked about fifty miles to the port city of Joppa, where he bought a ticket to Tarshish. Nobody today knows exactly where Tarshish was, but many scholars have the opinion that it was the city of Tartessus, which was in Spain. In any case it was a long way in a different direction from Nineveh.

So off Jonah went on a boat headed toward Tarshish. Before long God brought a great storm on the sea. The boat on which Jonah was a passenger was in serious danger of sinking. Now Jonah had made the mistake of telling some of the crew members that he was fleeing from his God. These crew members figured that if they tossed Jonah over the side into the raging sea, Jonah's God might let them off the hook, so to speak. At any rate it was worth a shot. Of course, Jonah knew he was the problem, so he swallowed hard and said, "Okay throw me overboard." And they did. Sure enough, the sea became calm.

There is an interesting side note to the story here. Chapter 1, verse 16 says that when this happened, the crew members became believers in Jonah's God—the one true God. Jonah's witness was in his failure. This is not the way we want to represent God. But God can use anything for the greater good.

Even though the sea was now calm, and the crew had become believers, they were not going to invite Jonah back onto the boat. They were believers, but they were not stupid. So there was Jonah treading water in the middle of the sea. He must have been wondering what would happen next. But I would bet that what did happen was not something he anticipated.

Chapter 1, verse 17 says that God had prepared a great fish to swallow Jonah. And Jonah spent the next three days and nights in the belly of this great fish. Sometimes this story is called Jonah and the whale. But Bible scholars tell is it was not a whale. A whale is a mammal, not a fish anyway. If the Bible says it was a fish, it was a fish. Now, this sounds like a very unpleasant experience to say the least. But consider this. Being swallowed by the fish was not to punish Jonah. It was to keep him from drowning and to give him a second chance to be obedient to God.

By the way, is this literally a true story about Jonah and the great fish? Well, I say that it is. I mentioned the Matthew 12 passage earlier, where Jesus refers to Jonah's being swallowed by the fish.

Jesus also used this story in His teachings in Matthew 16:4 and Luke 11:29–32. In all three passages, Jesus refers to this event as "the sign of Jonah," which is a call to repentance. In all three of these passages, Jesus used this "fish story" as an analogy to His own death and resurrection. He recognized it as an actual historic event. If Jesus said it happened, that is good enough for me. It happened.

Ah, but we have left Jonah in the belly of the fish. Let's get back there and see what happened next. Jonah spent those three fishy days and nights doing some very serious praying. He was saying, "Thank You, thank You, thank You, Lord, for saving me from drowning." And he also told God, "If you still want me to go to Nineveh, I will now certainly do just that."

So, in chapter 2, verse 10, the fish vomited Jonah onto dry land, thus illustrating the principle that it is hard to keep a prophet down. Then chapter 3 tells us that Jonah went to Nineveh. I hope he managed to shower first and find a fresh set of clothes. When he finally arrived in Nineveh, he walked through the city preaching history's shortest and most effective sermon. Troy translation here: "Listen up everybody, God is going to destroy this city in forty days unless you Ninevites repent. And I am glad of it!"

Well, much to Jonah's surprise, the people of Nineveh did repent. And God relented from destroying the city. Was Jonah happy about that? No, he was not. He still didn't think Nineveh should be spared. And so he missed the blessing. He was still an unhappy camper. He went off to sulk.

So, in chapter 4, God gave Jonah a lesson about grace. Even though Jonah eventually did what God assigned him to do, he did it with an ungracious heart. Let me take you to a New Testament passage, 2 Corinthians 9:7. It's the one the pastor uses on "Stewardship

Sunday" when his sermon focuses on the fact that church funds are short. It goes like this, "Let each one give as he purposes in his heart, not grudgingly or of necessity, for God loves a cheerful giver." Okay, that passage specifically refers to money. But I propose that it also refers to our time, our deeds, and our attitudes. We should be cheerful givers in all these areas, not just financial contributions. God treats us in grace; we really should be enthusiastic about treating others in grace. In that regard I commend a book for you. It is called *What's so Amazing about Grace?* It was written by Phillip Yancey back in the 1990s. But its principles are still valid. It is available online in hard copy or computer download. I got mine at amazon.com

Think for a minute about those three occasions when Jesus referred to the "Sign of Jonah." When He was doing these teachings, there were certainly Pharisees present. The Pharisees were ardent Old Testament scholars. They *knew* what Jesus meant when He used the three days in the fish story. He was making the point that He was (and is) the Messiah. He was seriously yanking the Pharisees' chains. He did that often in His teachings.

Now, let's look at the lessons in chapter 3.

Verse 1. God did not give up on Nineveh. God came to Jonah a second time to send him there.

Verse 2. God does not give up on Jonah. He once again told Jonah to go to Nineveh and preach His message to them.

Verse 3. Jonah arose and went to Nineveh. So what if it was a long way? If God sends us somewhere, He will provide the means to get there.

Verse 4. Jonah delivered God's message. Jonah did not need a team of writers. God gave Jonah the words he was to speak.

Verses 5 through 9. Nineveh repented. No nut is too tough for God to crack.

Verse 10. God had compassion on Nineveh. He did not destroy the city. He is a loving and compassionate God.

Now, some applications for us:

1. Just as God did not give up on Jonah, He does not give up on us. Even when we are disobedient, God will give us other chances to repent and obey. However, it is unwise to keep pushing back against God. He is infinite and eternal. But His patience is not. (See what happened in the Old Testament to pharaoh.)
2. We must recognize when God is giving us a chance to start over and be obedient. This comes when we realize: we need God, we need His forgiveness, *and* when God sends us to someone in need.
3. And that is the bottom line here. At some point in our lives, God is going to send each one of us to our own Nineveh. He will send us to minister in some way to somebody we do not like or consider deserving. So what do we do then? We obey God, but not grudgingly or of necessity. For God loves a cheerful giver—of time, of deeds, of finances, of self.

The Nike slogan is not biblical, but it fits here. If God tells you to do something, just do it!

CHAPTER 3

Batteries Not Included

Read 2 Corinthians 1:8–11.

In this brief passage, Paul tells the believers in the church at Corinth about his and Timothy's being delivered from death sentences while in Asia. The study notes in my Bible say that this illustrates that commitment to Christ does not exempt one from trouble. On the contrary, commitment to Christ is very likely, at some point, to cause one trouble.

By Asia here, Paul was referring to the Roman province of Asia Minor, which is modern day Turkey. Paul really got around on his missionary journeys! We are not told here exactly what caused him and Timothy to get in trouble serious enough to warrant being sentenced to death. But many Bible scholars think it was an event in Ephesus where a guy named Demetrius incited a riot against Paul for his preaching the gospel of Jesus Christ. This story is found in Acts 19:23–41. Demetrius was a silversmith. His principle business was making and selling pagan idols. Paul's preaching of Jesus was really cutting into his business. A lot of people in Ephesus made their living like that. So it would have been easy to start a riot with the idea of getting rid of these Christ-preaching troublemakers. And it was a big riot. God did deliver them, but they were in serious trouble for sure.

But back to our 2 Corinthians passage, in verse 11 Paul thanks the Corinthian believers for their prayers. Paul points out here that the more people become engaged in praying for other believers, the more people will be able to thank God for His prayer answers.

Some years ago Dr. Ron Allen, a professor of Hebrew at Dallas Theological Seminary, had a daughter who was about to undergo a very serious surgical procedure. The surgeon had already let Dr. Allen and his wife know that even one imprecise move in the surgical procedure could result in instant death for the young girl.

This doctor was a Christian believer. Just before he went into the operating room, he gathered the OR staff around the Allen family and suggested they all pray for success in the surgery. When the prayers were finished, this doctor turned to Dr. Allen and his wife and said, "You know it was really only necessary for one of us to pray here. But the reason I asked everybody to participate was so all of us could share the blessings of God's answer." Wow! What a great thought.

When I brought this lesson to my WFAA-TV Bible study, I told the group that they could just give me their prayer requests, and I could go off in a corner by myself and pray. But I always asked the group to pray silently as I prayed aloud, so we could all share the blessings of God's answers. There is no "Call Waiting" on God's prayer line. He doesn't need it. He can hear *all* our prayers simultaneously.

Okay, by now you are probably thinking, but what about the title of this study, "Batteries Not Included"? What is the connection? Well it is certainly a phase you have seen (or should have seen) countless times on boxes containing Christmas or birthday presents for kids in your families. Not noticing these words on the boxes can destroy Christmas, birthday, or any other gift-giving occasion.

These three words render useless even the most expensive and valuable gifts. Truly we want things to work when we hit the power switch. Think about all those years we saw the Energizer Bunny just keep going and going. But at some point even the strongest super-alkaline or Ni Cad batteries will run out of power. They were made by humans. And human power is limited, artificial, and temporary.

Aren't you glad that Jesus in John 14:16 said, "And I will pray the Father and He will give you another Helper that He may abide with you forever." The Holy Spirit really does just keep going and going. Notice that word *forever*. But we must acknowledge our human weakness before we can plug into God's Holy Spirit power outlet.

In Ephesians 6:10–11, Paul told the Ephesians, "Finally my brethren, be strong in the Lord and in the power of His might. Put on the whole armor of God that you may be able to stand against the wiles of the devil." Wouldn't you like to be able to do that? Well you can. But look at what Paul says in 2 Corinthians 12:5b, "I will not boast except in my infirmities (weaknesses)." What Paul is saying here is the only thing he has to brag about is that he is weak. Does that make sense? Yes, because we can only access God's power when we realize we have no power of our own.

As chapter 12 continues, Paul tells of asking God three times to remove his "thorn in the flesh." But God told Paul, "My grace is sufficient for you, for my strength is made perfect in (human) weakness." We don't know what that "thorn in the flesh" was. And it doesn't matter. It was certainly a potential distraction to Paul. God's words to Paul assuring him of His ample grace and power amounted to His telling Paul, "I got this." And in verse 10 Paul says, "Therefore I will take pleasure in infirmities, in reproaches, in needs, in persecutions, in distresses for Christ's sake. For when I am weak, then I am strong."

Paul had discovered that God would give him strength in direct relation to the degree that he admitted and experienced weakness. In the midst of his trials, he was able to rely on *divine* strength. If we fail to admit our weakness and keep on trying to deal with trials on our own, we absolutely turn off the power that God has available for us. It is human nature to do that. I do it. You do it. We all do it. We look at all the angles. Explore all the possibilities.

But, that is *not* the way it works. Only when we acknowledge to God our weakness, our helplessness, can we access God's power. When we finally do this, God says, "I have been waiting for you to put your complete dependence on Me. Here's My power." There are just no man-made batteries like that!

CHAPTER 4

What's Up with That Red Bible?

I am a graduate of Baylor University, which is a major training ground for Baptist preachers. So I was around a lot of these young guys during my years there. I sometimes think of one of them in particular. His name was Teddy Charles ... something. I don't remember his last name. After all, this was over fifty years ago. But, Teddy Charles, if you are reading this, you know who you are.

One evening after dinner Teddy Charles came over to the off-campus house where I lived with several other guys. He was really excited. The night before, he had watched a Billy Graham Crusade service on TV. Something Dr. Graham said prompted him to immediate action. He went out the next morning as soon as the stores opened and made a purchase—a new Bible, but not just any Bible. It was bound in bright red leather. He came bursting into our living room and shouted, "Billy Graham said last night that every Bible should be *red*!"

Well, maybe most of us are not quite as goofy as Teddy Charles (He was fond of jumping out from behind parked cars in front of our house to frighten approaching drivers). But we all do need to pay attention to what Billy Graham actually said that night. The spelling is very important. Dr. Graham said every Bible should be *read*. A Bible may look official on your coffee table, in your bookcase, or in your office at work. But unless you actually pick it up and *read* it, it is just window dressing.

We used to have a cat. His name was Gus. I would often come into the kitchen and find Gus sitting on the morning newspaper. That is the way a lot of folks treat the Bible. You can't absorb it by osmosis. Gus never learned anything about the Bible. Neither will you if you use it for a seat cushion.

Consider Hebrews 4:12, which says, "For the Word of God is living and powerful, sharper than any two edged sword, piercing even to the division of the soul and the spirit, and of joints and marrow, and is a discerner of the thoughts and intents of the heart." Wow! Powerful stuff! But, guess what. A sword is totally ineffective if it is in a scabbard or behind glass in a display case. You have to use the sword to divide the soul and the spirit and the joints and the marrow. You have to read the Bible in order for it to be a discerner of the thoughts and intents of your heart. Look at Psalm 119. Verse 11 says, "Your Word I have hidden in my heart." Verse 12b says, "Teach me Your statutes." And verse 15 says, "I will meditate on Your precepts and contemplate Your ways."

The Hebrew word for statutes is boundaries. The Bible is God's Word. God's precepts are His divine principles. And the word *meditate* means to go over something again and again in your mind. God wants us to take the opportunity of seeking Him by reading His Book. And life is short. We only have a limited time to do that. Isaiah 55:6 emphasizes that. It says, "Seek the Lord while He may be found. Call upon Him while He is near."

Second Corinthians 10:4–6 tell us that as Christians, our weapons are not carnal (worldly), "but mighty in God, for pulling down strongholds, casting down arguments and every high thing that exalts itself against the knowledge of God, bringing every thought into captivity to the obedience of Christ." Again, powerful stuff, but only when put to use.

Developing a discipline of reading the Bible every day is the first step on the right path. You might start with just a few minutes a day. But the *every* day thing is important. Reading the Bible regularly is the beginning of establishing a relationship with God. If you do this, before you know it, when problems arise in your life, you will realize that you know where to go to get the answers. But only when you have the knowledge of the Word of God in your heart, can the Holy Spirit come alongside you to remind you of the appropriate truth to apply to your crisis.

The value of God's Word simply cannot be measured. Not only is it a guide for our lives, but it shows us the way into God's heart. Is that too abstract a concept? Well, it just means, that God is pleased when we do what He wants us to do. And that begins with a desire to do what His Word says in our every circumstance.

The Holy Spirit—our divine Helper—is always available to us to point us to the truths we need to get through any situation. But in order for the Holy Spirit to point us to the appropriate statutes, precepts, and commandments, we have to have read them and learned them. You have to know God's Word before you can keep it.

Every Bible should be read. Any color is okay.

CHAPTER 5

Turn Your Radio On

That's the title of a great old Statler Brothers gospel song. The lyrics speak of a "radio station where the mighty hosts of heaven sing." And the payoff line at the end of each verse is, "Get in touch with God. Turn your radio on."

Have you ever been driving between cities trying to listen on the radio to a game involving a favorite team? You sometimes have to adjust the frequency over and over as you drive along. You keep your ears cocked to pick up through the static the familiar voice of the announcer for your team.

Our Christian lives are like that. We need to be persistent in adjusting the frequencies in our minds to hear God's voice. And it is often hard to keep from being distracted by other voices or just the static of life.

Is it always possible to tune in to God's voice? John 10:27 says it is. Jesus says, "My sheep hear My voice, and I know them, and they follow Me." And while we are in this passage, the next couple of verses give us as Christians our promise of eternal security. That is to say, once you become a Christian believer, you cannot lose your

Jesus Makes Salsa by the Seashore

salvation and eternal life, even if later you disavow Christianity! We might change our minds. God does not. God is unchanging.

John 10:28–29 says, "And I give them (His sheep / believers) eternal life and they shall never perish; neither shall anyone snatch them out of My hand. My Father, who has given them to Me, is greater than all; and no one is able to snatch them out of My Father's hand. My Father and I are one." Eternal security is not the principle subject of our study here. But how reassuring it is to be reminded that we do have it!

But back to, "Get in touch with God. Turn your radio on." Continuing that radio metaphor, what are some of the conditions to tuning in to God's voice?

1. You have to be in range of His voice. How do you stay in range? Stay close to where God's voice is being "broadcast." You can pick up God's voice in reading the Bible and attending (and paying attention in) church or Bible studies. If you are not where God's voice is being broadcast, all you get is polka music
2. And this goes right along with being in range. You have to make sure you are tuned to the right channel. Compare whatever it is you are listening to in your life with the standards taught in the Bible.
3. Be willing to adjust your dial. Often what God says will conflict with what seems logical to our human minds. So don't assume the voice you hear is not God because what it says disagrees with your preconceived notions. We need to align ourselves with His program.

There is a very good Bible study course that was done by Canadian preacher, teacher, and evangelist Henry Blackaby. It's called Experiencing God. I highly recommend it. There is a book. And there is a fill in the blanks study guide to accompany the book. You should be able to find both in your Christian bookstore or online.

Henry Blackaby has a prayer in this study that is just dynamite. We should all have a copy of it on our refrigerators or bathroom mirrors to remind us to pray it every day. This is my paraphrase of the prayer:

> Dear God, please grant that I hear Your voice, understand the necessary adjustments I must make to get into Your will; that I make those adjustments, in Your power, not my own, and be obedient to You.

Now, that's a tuning in to God's voice prayer.

Sometimes we hear God's voice, but we don't recognize it. Or, we don't realize He is talking to *us*. This happened to the prophet (and the last of the Judges) Samuel when he was a young boy. The story is in 1 Samuel 3:1–21. God spoke to Samuel, wakening him from sleep. But Samuel thought it was his mentor Eli calling from the next-door bedroom. This happened three times. Finally Eli realized it was God calling to Samuel. He told the youngster to go back to his room and listen. "If God calls you again," Eli said, "say, Speak Lord, for your servant hears." Well, God did call to Samuel again. And Samuel answered, "Speak, for your servant hears."

What God told Samuel was that he was to inform Eli that his life was to be taken because he did not restrain the behavior of his two sons who practiced evil. Of course, Samuel did not want to give Eli that bad news. But the next morning he did. And Eli told Samuel he had done the right thing by following God's instructions.

Now Samuel didn't ask God to speak to him. God initiated the conversation. Should we ever ask God to speak to us? Yes, but be careful. We should not ask God to speak to us until we are ready to make a commitment to do whatever God tells us to do. When we are ready to make that commitment, and we ask God to speak to us, believe it or not, He will.

But, if you ask God to give you instructions and He does, and you don't follow through on them, you are *really* asking for trouble. Proverbs 20:25 addresses this: "It is a snare for a man to devote rashly something as holy, and afterward reconsider his vows."

And God's voice might well speak to us in rebuke or correction about something we are doing or not doing. In Proverbs 1:23 God tells us, "Turn at my rebuke." That means when God corrects you, pay attention and turn in the direction God is guiding you. Proverbs 3:11 says, "My son, do not despise the chastening of the Lord, nor detest His correction. For whom the Lord loves He corrects, just as the father the son in whom he delights." No one knows for sure who wrote Hebrews, but the author used a paraphrase of this Proverb in Hebrews 12:6. Double emphasis!

So, restating Henry Blackaby's prayer in the plural, so as to include all of us:

> Dear God, please grant that we hear Your voice, understand the adjustments we must make in our lives to get into Your plan, make those adjustments, in Your power not our own, and be obedient to You.

Get in touch with God. Turn your (spiritual) radio on!

CHAPTER 6

Spiritual Fruit Checkers

Read Matthew 12:1–14.

It seems as though Jesus was always doing something on the Sabbath to get under the skin of the Pharisees. First, in this passage He and His disciples were walking through a field of grain on a Sabbath. The disciples were hungry. So they began to pluck some heads of grain and eat them (a health food snack). There were usually some Pharisees hanging around Jesus and His disciples checking up on them. This day was no exception. When the Pharisees saw this, they got really bent out of shape and took it up with Jesus.

Well, okay, there is that commandment number four in the Ten Commandments where God told the Israelites through Moses that they were to remember the Sabbath day and keep it holy. It also said that no work was to be performed on the Sabbath. Well, first Jesus gave these Pharisees a couple of biblical examples where both David and priests of the temple picked and ate grain on the Sabbath. But then He really nailed them. He told them that the Son of Man (one of Jesus's favorite names for Himself) was greater than the temple, and He was Lord even of the Sabbath. That really yanked the Pharisees' chain.

So I mentioned the fourth commandment, which is in the Mosaic Law. The Mosaic Law was the ideal, but it was an impossible standard. The Israelites, being human, could never keep all its statutes. That is why God set up one day a year as the Day of Atonement—Yom Kippur. On that day the temple priests would offer sacrifices that would cover the sins of the people for that year. But this had to be done every year. It was a foreshadowing of the time when Messiah would come and take care of all sin permanently.

Jesus "working" on the Sabbath by picking grain and then saying He was Lord even of the Sabbath was really saying, "Messiah is here. You are no longer under the law. You now have freedom in Me." He was telling them if He said something was okay, then it was okay.

The Pharisees, however, kept strict devotion to the law, what we could call legalism. But legalism drains compassion for others. Jesus told the Pharisees here in verse 7 that He desired mercy, not sacrifice. Well, these Pharisees knew the Old Testament inside out. When Jesus said that, they knew He was going back to Proverbs 21:3: "To do righteousness and justice is more desirable to the Lord than sacrifice." This meant He was identifying Himself as God. The Pharisees *really* couldn't handle that.

The sacrifices mentioned in the Proverbs passage and by Jesus here represent the law. Jesus had just told them that He superseded the law. But in their blind devotion to the law, the Pharisees couldn't (or more likely wouldn't) take that in. The Pharisees here represent several things, all of which we should be aware of and avoid.

1. We have already noted that legalism drains one's compassion for others. Observation of law should be tempered with mercy.
2. Legalism blinds judgment. Later on that same Sabbath day, Jesus healed a man with a withered hand. Once again the Pharisees got on His case. He gave them an example of how it would be all right to rescue a sheep that fell into a pit on the Sabbath. In their clouded judgment based in legalism, the passage then says that they (the Pharisees) went out and began plotting against Jesus that they might kill Him.
3. Legalism promotes hypocrisy. The Pharisees' interpretation of the law allowed for the rescue of a sheep on the Sabbath, but not healing a man's withered hand.
4. Legalism keeps one from rejoicing in someone's doing something for the benefit of others.

Not only were the Pharisees steeped in legalism and hypocrisy, their attempts at being spiritual "fruit checkers" of the things Jesus was doing had begun to show them that Jesus was becoming a real threat to their positions of authority. Thus we see the beginning of their plot to get rid of Him.

But what can we take away from this study in our own lives? Here are a couple of things. It is not our job as Christians to be spiritual "fruit checkers." God did not put us here to judge what other people are doing. I am reminded of an incident that occurred when George W. Bush was making his first run for the presidency. He was, at that time, governor of Texas. The question of his position on homosexuality had become an "elephant in the room." It fell to Doug Fox, one of my colleagues at WFAA-TV in Dallas, to ask him about this issue. In a TV interview, Doug asked him, "Governor, do you believe homosexuality is a sin?" Bush's answer, "Doug, we're all sinners in need of redemption."

No matter what you think of former President Bush, I propose to you that that was a great answer, because it is so true.

The other thing I will note here is that being a spiritual fruit checker is certain to cause one to be blind to his own sin. That is a real danger.

We are not to let things we infer from Scripture be standards we hold for others. We are only responsible for our own standards. We should not dwell on disagreements. In our relationships with other Christian believers, we need only agree that Jesus Christ is the Son of God, and therefore He is God Himself. And as God, He came to earth and died on a cross, taking on Himself punishment for all human sin, past, present, and future. Then three days later He conquered death, arising from the grave to provide eternal life to all who believe in Him.

Everything else is small stuff.

CHAPTER 7

We're in a Tight Spot!

Read Genesis 22:1–14.

Back in 2000 there was a movie called *Oh Brother, Where Art Thou?* It was a hilarious farce starring George Clooney as an escaped convict. It won an Oscar for best writing based on material previously produced or published. That categorization came because it was based on a very unlikely source, Homer's epic poem *The Odyssey.* If you haven't seen this movie, you should.

What has this got to do with this Bible lesson? Well, really, not much.

It's just that all through this film, as Clooney's character and his not-so-bright companions were placed in one impossible situation after another, the response of Clooney's character was, "We're in a tight spot!"

I kept thinking about that phrase as I wrote this study. Both of the people in this Bible story might well have used this phrase more than once regarding the situation in which God had placed them.

So what's going on here in Genesis 22:1–14? God had promised Abraham in chapter 17 that He would make him the father of many nations. But, God's timing is often not what we would like it to be. That was the case with Abraham and his wife Sarah. God made them wait a *long* time for the heirs to be born to father these nations. Among these many nations would be all the Arab countries, whose people are descended from Ishmael. But the Jews, God's chosen people, would have to descend from Isaac, Abraham's only legitimate son. Isaac was a miracle baby, born when Abraham was one hundred years old and Sarah was ninety. And the instructions God gave Abraham here in chapter 22 certainly made it seem that Isaac was not going to be around to father anybody.

In this chapter, God came to Abraham with a real test. In verses 1 and 2 God told Abraham to take his only legitimate son, and heir, up a mountain in the land of Moriah and offer him there as a burnt offering. And the text then says that Abraham got up early in the morning, saddled his donkey, gathered two of his young men and Isaac, and headed for the mountain carrying wood he had split for a fire.

Now *that* was a test. It was a huge test of Abraham's faith. God wanted him to kill his only legitimate son? But Abraham didn't question God or protest what God told him to do. He just did it. It took two and a half days for them to get to the place of the sacrifice. So Abraham had plenty of time to say to himself, "We're in a tight spot!"

Okay, let's personalize this. In what tight spot has God placed you? What's going on in your life that has you desperately searching for a solution? We all have tight spots—certainly not as tight as this one. But God does test our faith. So what is your tight spot response? Denial is one way you might go. Ignore the situation, and maybe it will go away. It won't. Of course, you might say, "Well I don't have any situation like that in my life." That could mean one of two things. One is that God knows you don't have enough faith to pass a test, and He is giving you a chance to mature. Or He may already have the perfect storm coming at you around the next corner. You just don't see it yet.

God *does* test us. He *does* put us in tight spots. These situations are our chances to grow spiritually. These situations require us to put our confidence in God. We need to learn from Abraham. In verses 3 through 8 he demonstrates absolute confidence in God in a spot that could hardly be tighter.

But, meanwhile, what must have been going on in Isaac's mind? Here he was going up to the mountain with his dad. He was observing that among the supplies his dad had are a rope, some split wood, no doubt he had coals of fire, and he had a big sharp knife. So what was this sacrifice to be? They seemed to be missing a sheep. Isaac surely realized that he was the likely candidate to be the burnt offering. He too was probably whispering, "We're in a tight spot." But just as Abraham had full confidence in God, his heavenly Father, Isaac demonstrated full confidence in Abraham, his earthly father.

Both of them were prepared to follow God's instructions even though they made no sense from a human viewpoint. God will often give us directions that violate our human common sense. In those cases, we want God's blessing, but we don't want His direction. But if we obey His directions and follow up by seeking guidance in His Word, the Bible, we can find comfort as we obey Him. Psalm 119:105 says, "Your Word is a lamp unto my feet and a light unto my path."

Every time we respond to God's direction by making a right decision, we open the door for God to reveal to us the next step He wants us to take. When we make a wrong decision, we shut down the process and neutralize our effectiveness for God.

We should probably tape 2 Timothy 3:16–17 on our bathroom mirrors or refrigerator doors so that we will see the verses every day. "All scripture is given by inspiration of God and is profitable for doctrine, for reproof, for correction, for instruction in righteousness, that the man (or woman) of God may be complete, thoroughly equipped for every good work."

God *will* give us directions and He *will* give us guidance *if* we seek those directions and that guidance in His Word. Then, having found His directions and guidance, we must focus on them, not allowing anything to distract us from God's plan for our lives. That's what Abraham and Isaac did. As the moment of the sacrifice approached, Abraham didn't panic. Isaac didn't panic. In this tightest of tight spots, they both surrendered their wills to God. And they had peace.

In verses 9 and 10, Abraham laid Isaac on the altar and raised his knife to kill him. But in verses 11 and 12, an angel of the Lord called out from heaven and told Abraham not to harm Isaac. Then, in verse 13, Abraham saw that God had provided a ram caught in some nearby bushes. And he offered the ram as the burnt offering. Abraham's faith was confirmed. So was Isaac's. God was pleased.

Of course, all of the animal sacrifices in the Old Testament foreshadow and point to the ultimate sacrifice, Jesus Christ. We are all sinners. We all deserve to die. God provided that ram to spare Isaac. But that was only a symbol of what was to come. Jesus gave Himself as a sacrifice for us. He alone could do that, because He was (and is) God. And He was (and is) man. And yet as man He was without sin. Only He could qualify to take our sins on Himself in our place. He died on the cross for that purpose. But then He rose from death that we might have eternal life *if* we believe in Him.

Our bottom line tight spot is that as humans we are condemned sinners. But Acts 16:31 gives us the way of deliverance from eternal punishment: "Believe on the Lord Jesus Christ and you will be saved."

Our tight spots are tests, of course. But they provide opportunities to trust in God. As James 1:2–3 tells us, "My brethren, count it all joy when you fall into various trials, knowing that the testing of your faith produces patience." And the word here for patience can also be translated endurance.

CHAPTER 8

The Blivet Principle

For thirty-one years I was the chief weather anchor at WFAA-TV in Dallas-Fort Worth. I can't count the times during those years that, as I walked over to the anchor desk to begin the weathercast, the floor director would relay a message from the producer in the control room, "Quick weather lead!" This meant, of course, that the newscast was running over schedule. There was going to be too much content to fit into allotted time. It was overfilled.

We called this "the blivet principle." You know what a blivet is? One of my dictionaries says it is an optical illusion or an impossible object. The other doesn't list the word at all. But in my context, it comes from an old military slang word. I will have to change the language a bit, but you'll get the idea. It means ten pounds of manure in a five-pound bag."

And can't our lives get like that?

The world around us continues to stress achieving more, doing more, being more. We can easily become trapped in a never-ending cycle of activity—like a hamster in a wheel, running and running and running—trying unsuccessfully to catch up with life.

It is like the old saying, "I understand that God will not let me die until I have done everything He set out for me to do. I'm so far behind I may live forever!" Well, of course God doesn't work like that. But it does express the frustration we often feel.

What we really need to do is pull over to the curb and rest—in Christ. In Mark 6:31, Jesus tells His disciples to come away with Him by themselves and rest for a while. At this point Jesus has just sent them all over Israel to preach the gospel of repentance. Repent means literally to change one's mind. In context here, it means to come to belief that the promised Messiah had arrived in the person of Jesus. He had told them to travel light, not even taking food or a change of clothes. This was to encourage them to put their trust in God for the fulfillment of all their needs. They went out and preached the gospel of Jesus and cast out demons. Jesus had given them power over what He called unclean spirits. They also anointed with oil many who were sick and healed them.

When they all got back to give Jesus their reports, they were no doubt exhausted. So that's when Jesus, in Mark 6:31, told them to come away with Him to get some rest. So they all got in a boat and pushed out into the Sea of Galilee for a little R&R, or so they thought.

But remember what happened next? The multitudes saw them take off in the boat and ran to be where Jesus and the disciples would be landing across the lake. Mark 6:34 then says that Jesus saw all these people and had compassion on them. He told the guys to pull over to shore, and He started to teach all these folks in what was now a huge crowd. In fact this is the occasion of the feeding of the five thousand. But it was more likely closer to ten thousand, since the Greek here says five thousand men. There were probably at least an equal number of women and children.

You will no doubt remember that Jesus told the disciples to get all these people some food, since it was now late in the day, and none of them had eaten. Well, the disciples got all bent out of shape. No doubt they were thinking (and probably saying), "What kind of rest is this? This is not rest. Jesus just gave us an impossible task." Their circuits were overloaded. They were frustrated by their inability to do what needed to be done. They were each being assigned to carry a blivet.

The trouble was that they had misinterpreted the word *rest*. He meant that they were to rest in Him—trust Him to provide them with a way to do whatever He had asked them to do. He would have a plan. Well, of course he did have a plan. And you know the rest of the story. The small boy had five loaves of bread and two fish, which amply fed the thousands of hungry people. *And* there were twelve baskets of leftovers.

So how does this Bible story apply to us? We need to ask ourselves if all our running in the hamster wheel activity is something necessary that God chose for us to do. Well, it is not. Psalm 46:10 tells us, "Be still and know that I am God." He wants us to slow down and realize that our lives are in His hands. When we do, we replace striving with resting and trusting in God. Does that mean we slack off on our jobs at work? No, it does not. But it does mean that we put all our excess baggage on God. Too much work, too little time, boss driving you nuts? Give those things to God. Give your best effort. Then rest in Him. Psalm 55:22 says, "Cast your burden on the Lord and He will sustain you. He shall never permit the righteous to be moved."

There is a great illustration of the solution to the blivet principle problem in a 1986 movie starring the British actor Jeremy Irons. It is called *The Mission*. Irons's character Mendoza has been a slave trader. Now he is overcome with guilt and decides he must

35

do penance for his sins. As his chosen penance, he is struggling to climb a steep, slippery mountain while carrying on his back a huge and heavy pack full of armor and weapons from his former life. Near the peak of the mountain, he comes to a ridge that he comes to realize will be impassable. He can't move the heavy pack another inch no matter how he tries. At this point, he suddenly sees a young native boy coming toward him carrying a large machete.

Mendoza thinks, *Well this is it. This boy is going to kill me. But at least I will be out of my misery.* However, the boy has something else in mind. With a stroke of his razor-sharp machete, the young boy cuts the heavy pack from Mendoza's back, sending it crashing down the mountain into a deep ravine. The two are unable to communicate verbally. But they fall into an embrace as Mendoza breaks into tears of gratitude and relief.

Like Mendoza, we all have sin in our lives. But God does not ask us to carry its weight on our backs. He does not even ask us to do penance for our wrongdoings. Instead He sent His Son, Jesus, to bear not only our sins, but the sins of the entire world—past, present, and future.

And John 3:16 says, "Whoever believes in Him (Jesus) will not perish, but have eternal life."

And regarding our sins, they are already forgiven. But when we sin, we take ourselves out of fellowship with God. That is to say, we neutralize our Christian witness. First John 1:9 tells us what to do when we mess up. It says all we have to do is confess our sins to God, and He is faithful and just to forgive us those sins (the specific ones we confess) and cleanse us from all unrighteousness (the ones we didn't even mention).

Is there a blivet in your life? Are you carrying around ten pounds of manure in a five-pound bag? God will cut that bag loose and let it slide down into the ravine *if* you let Him.

I love Philippians 4:13: "I can do all things through Christ who strengthens me."

CHAPTER 9

This Is What the Captain Meant ...

When I graduated from Baylor University, my first TV job out of college was doing news at KBTX-TV in Bryan, Texas. While I was there, I developed a special friendship with three other guys at the station who were about my age. Before long we started a little musical group called the Festoons. We played together a couple of years before we all went our separate ways. But through the years we have maintained our friendships, even though in far different locations. Toby Hughes played a ukulele. Bob Huffaker played bongos. Billy Arhos played guitar. And I played a bass fiddle made from a lard can attached to a broom with a piece of clothesline. Hard to believe, but it really worked.

I had a long career in television weather, the last thirty-one years in Dallas. Billy Arhos had a great career in television that included creating and producing the long-running show *Austin City Limits*. Bob Huffaker was a TV reporter in Dallas in 1963. He was standing about six feet away when Jack Ruby shot Lee Harvey Oswald. After television, Bob went on to a long career as an educator. Toby Hughes became a career officer in the US Air

Force. He had an outstanding record as a fighter pilot. Toby flew over a hundred combat missions in Vietnam in F-4 aircraft.

We had a Festoons reunion many years later, in 1996. Toby brought a number of songs he had written while serving in Vietnam. My favorite was called "This Is What the Captain Meant." It described the daily briefing, when the captain would assemble all the men (no women at the time) and give them their orders for the day. When the captain finished, he would turn things over to the sergeant and leave. The men had heard what the captain had to say. But at this point, the sergeant would turn to them and say, "You heard what the captain said. Now, this is what the captain meant."

We often need somebody like that to come to us after we have read a passage in the Bible, don't we? Here are a couple of examples where the Old Testament Scriptures of Judaism can help explain the meaning of New Testament passages.

For instance, look at John 7:37–38: "On the last day, that great day of the feast, Jesus stood and cried out, 'If anyone thirsts, let him come to Me and drink. He who believes in Me, as the Scripture has said, out of his heart will flow rivers of living water.'"

Well, here's the background: In ancient Israel, on the last day of the Feast of the Tabernacles in Jerusalem, a priest took a golden pitcher and went out of the city walls to the Pool of Siloam. The priest would draw a pitcher of water and bring it back to the temple. He would then pour the water out as an offering to God, commemorating the water that God had caused to flow from the rock back when the Israelites were wandering through the wilderness. But here's the kicker. Here is what the priest would do as he poured out the water. He would lift his eyes to heaven and pray to God, "Lord, send us your Messiah now."

It was at this precise moment in the service when Jesus stood and cried out the words in John 7:37–38. He was saying, "You asked for it! You got it! Your Messiah is here! Here I am! I am the source of the rivers of living water!" It was the perfect situation for Jesus to identify Himself as the Messiah. And He did.

Another "This is what the captain meant" moment occurs in John chapter 8 when the Pharisees brought the woman caught in adultery to Jesus to see if they could trip Him up over what punishment she should receive. Consider what Jesus did just before He delivered that famous line, "He who is without sin among you, let him throw a stone at her first."

He stooped down and wrote something in the dirt with His finger. The study notes in my Bible say that what He wrote is a matter of conjecture, perhaps the Ten Commandments. But go back to the Old Testament, to Jeremiah 17:13. God tells Jeremiah the prophet, "Those who depart from Me shall be written in the earth, because they have forsaken the Lord, the fountain of living waters." That is just how Jesus had identified Himself in the previous chapter, at which we just looked—the source of living waters. Looks to me as if Jesus was "taking names."

This is perhaps a nontraditional interpretation. But I think it is valuable because I got it from a Messianic rabbi. You may already know that Messianic Jews maintain their Jewish heritage. But they believe in and worship Yeshua (Jesus) as the Messiah. They often use Old Testament Scriptures to help explain New Testament Scriptures.

You might want to seek out a Messianic temple near where you live. They generally have materials for distribution that can help Christians use Old Testament Scriptures to reveal to their Jewish friends that Jesus is indeed the Messiah. There are over three hundred prophecies in the Old Testament regarding the Messiah. Jesus fulfilled them *all*. No one else in history fulfilled even a few.

So, this is what "the captain" meant: No doubt about it, Jesus *is* the Messiah.

CHAPTER 10

Don't Be Stingy with Your Hugs

In 1 Thessalonians 3:12, the apostle Paul, praying for the Christian believers in the church at Thessaloniki, says, "And may the Lord make you increase and abound in love to one another."

There are at least nine passages in the New Testament in which we Christian believers are instructed to love one another. The strongest of these is the command by Jesus Himself in John 13:34–35. He called it a new commandment. But it is so strong that it has come to be called the Great Commandment. In this passage, Jesus tells us that we should love each other as He loved us. And how did he love us? He gave His life for us in His death on the cross. This is a heavy-duty commandment for us.

Here Paul is reinforcing this thought to the Thessalonian believers (and to us). Paul prays here in 1 Thessalonians 4 that we would love each other more and more. To follow these apostolic instructions, we need to actively look for ways to manifest the love of Christ by touching other people's lives with our love, to be free with our love.

How freely do we love others? Do we give our love without expecting something in return? We all want to be loved. We all need to be loved. In Acts 20:35 Luke quotes Jesus as saying, "It is more blessed to give than to receive." This saying from Jesus is not actually found in the Gospels. But Luke here indicates a knowledge of His saying it. And the principle is sound.

Now it is important not to twist this around A friend of mine once told me that as Christmas approached that year, his wife told him that he should remember that it is more blessed to give too much, than to receive too little. She was kidding, of course. She knew the real principle. But most of us tend to be like that, don't we? It is natural human instinct to think that the three most important things in life are me, me, and me. This is the exact opposite of the truth.

Now, a personal story. Some years ago, just before Thanksgiving, a couple we knew was beginning the process of getting a divorce. Although we considered them both to be friends, we were much closer to the woman than the man. Thus we invited the woman to have Thanksgiving dinner at our house with us and another couple who were also mutual friends. This woman said that she would love to do that, but she was concerned about her estranged husband spending Thanksgiving alone. So she asked us if we would invite him in her place. She had several other invitations for Thanksgiving. But she knew that he did not.

This seemed at first to be a bit bizarre to the four of us. We didn't really know this guy that well. And what we did know about him was that he was very quiet and reserved. We were not excited at this prospect. But ...

That day I was preparing the lesson for the weekly Bible study I did at WFAA-TV. So I thought, well, I will prepare the study and then think about what to do about this Thanksgiving situation. So that is what I did. But when I finished my lesson, I decided to check the mail. One piece caught my eye. It was a newsletter from a Christian missionary in Colombia whom we supported. And at the time of this writing we still support him and his wife, although they are now teaching at a Bible school in South Texas. I read the letter, and everything changed.

This missionary's name is David Love. Here is what he had to say in that newsletter:

> Last night I spent a good part of the evening with a brother and sister (in their late 20's) who spend most of the time on the streets here in Bogota. They watch parked cars and earn about $3.00 dollars a day. I just sat on the side of the road in front of a Catholic Church in the chilly evening and listened to them. I didn't say a lot.
>
> They went into great detail as to how their dad came home every night and beat them. They called their Father "the Nazi." The brother, whose name is David, is quite intelligent, but only has a third grade education. It was almost 9 PM, and I really needed to get off the streets and get home. As I stood up, David came over to me and hugged me. He squeezed hard and wouldn't let go. Feeling a tad embarrassed, I knew that David had probably never been hugged before in his whole life. I determined not to be the first to pull away.
>
> Thanks for praying for us in this needy country. Gotta run to class. It is interesting, a couple of pastors whom I teach also give me hugs every day. I wonder if they had dads that hugged them.

I am not ashamed to admit that when I put down that newsletter, I had tears in my eyes. (What do you know? As I write this, many years later, my eyes are moist again).

I knew then what I was supposed to do.

Now in most ways the fellow I was asked to invite for Thanksgiving bore no resemblance to those young people on the streets of Bogota. In fact he was a very successful businessman in Dallas. But his estranged wife was sensitive to the fact that he was in need of at least a figurative hug. And Janet and I and the other couple who were to be there had those to give.

Well, I telephoned this fellow and invited him for Thanksgiving. I could tell by his voice on the phone that he was genuinely touched and happy to be included in our celebration. In fact I found out later that as soon as he hung up from our conversation, he phoned his estranged wife and told her how pleased he was to be invited to our house for this occasion.

He came to our house that Thursday, had Thanksgiving dinner with us, and stayed for about five hours. We had a great day. I was scheduled to work that evening. (TV weather goes on even if it is a holiday.) So I had to leave at 2:00 p.m. He was sitting on one of our living room couches. I went over to shake hands with him and tell him good-bye. But when I got there, I bent down and gave him a hug. And he hugged me back.

How we love others reflects the love we have for Jesus. No act of love is wasted. Shame on me for having to get a spiritual kick in the pants from my friend David Love to wake up and smell the coffee. But thank You, Lord, for providing it.

Don't be stingy with your hugs.

CHAPTER 11

Slam!

That's the symbolic sound of an emphatically closed door. We all experience this frustrating situation from time to time. Paul, Silas, Timothy, and Luke did too.

Acts 16:6–7 says, "Now when they had gone through Phrygia and the region of Galatia, they were forbidden by the Holy Spirit to preach the Word in Asia. And after they had come to Mysia, they tried to go into Bithynia, but the Holy Spirit did not permit them." There is no question that God has the power to open any door. No circumstances are too difficult for Him. But He may decide to let some things that seem very important to us be blocked from our access. Why does the Lord slam doors?

1. Protection. He often closes doors to us to prevent us from making mistakes. On our own we might not have adequate knowledge to make right choices. I am reminded of that wonderful old movie *The Magnificent Seven*. Yul Brenner's and Steve McQueen's characters had signed on to what looked like the impossible job of protecting a village from a really bad guy and his gang. One of the

other characters asked Steve McQueen why they had done it. McQueen's character said it was like the man who jumped into a cactus patch. When asked why he did that, he replied, "It seemed like a good idea at the time." God knows best. He does not want us to jump on a cactus.

2. Redirection. When God closes a door to us, it might be because He is sending us on a new path, maybe one that we would never have considered on our own. His plan might include bigger opportunities than we would allow ourselves to consider. These might be opportunities for broader service, greater productivity, and deeper satisfaction than we could imagine. Now His redirection plan for us could include suffering. But suffering builds the strength of character we need to take on whatever is behind the door God does open.

3. Testing. God might be giving us the opportunity to decide what we really believe about Him and whether we trust Him or not. First Corinthians 10:13 tells us that God will not tempt us to trials that are too much for us to handle, *if* we trust completely in Him.

4. Timing. He can sometimes close doors temporarily. His answer to our prayer request might be, "Not no, but not now." His timing is not our timing. Such occasions are opportunities to show patience, and to wait upon the Lord.

5. Perseverance. This is related to patience. You might say it is a by-product of patience. Romans 5:3–5 says, "We also glory in tribulations, knowing that tribulation produces perseverance, and perseverance character, and character hope (or confidence)."

6. Disobedience. When we find our way blocked, we need to ask ourselves if we are being disobedient to God by pursuing something that is just not in His plan.

How did Paul, Silas, Timothy, and Luke respond when God said no to their plan to go and preach the gospel in Asia? Well, being human, they first tried a plan B. They headed for a place called Bithynia. But the Holy Spirit blocked that plan too. So Paul took his guys in the only direction left open, northwest. He saw a divine vision that told him they were finally on the right track. The Holy Spirit guided them to Macedonia, where the Lord wanted them to go to preach the gospel.

How do we respond to closed doors? Well, Paul and the guys got it almost right. They needed a little more patience at first. Then, having persevered, they went the direction God wanted them to go. If we do as well as they did, we are ahead of the game. We also, being human, will probably try a plan B. But once it becomes clear that the doors we want are not the ones God wants, we are to practice patience and perseverance. Then God *will* direct us to another door. Our proper response, of course, is to follow His directions (preferably without proposing our own plan B).

Here is the guide God gave us. Philippians 4:6–7 says, "Be anxious for nothing, but in everything, by prayer and supplication, with thanksgiving, let your requests be made known to God; and the peace of God, which surpasses all understanding will guard your hearts and minds through Christ Jesus." You see what that means? Sure, make prayer requests to God. But if the answer is no or just silence, put your trust in Him and await further instructions.

When God closes doors to us, we must practice some "don'ts."

1. Don't push ahead anyway by manipulating our circumstances to try to make it look like whatever we are going to do is okay with God.
2. Don't become emotionally unglued and replace our Christ-centered perspective with a self-centered perspective.

3. Don't try to blame somebody else for our failure to open a door. *And* especially don't get angry at God over the situation.

And there are a few "dos" we need to practice.

1. Do wait on the Lord and trust Him. Proverbs 3:5–6 says, "Trust in the Lord with all your heart and lean not on your own understanding. In all your ways acknowledge Him and He shall direct your paths."
2. Do continually pray for guidance. Pray for sensitivity and understanding. First Thessalonians 5:17 says, "Pray without ceasing."
3. Do anticipate that God will open the right doors for us. Jeremiah 29:11 says, "For I know the thoughts I have toward you, says the Lord, thoughts of peace and not of evil, to give you a future and a hope."
4. Do thank God for His work on our behalf. Even if we are having a hard time finding something to be thankful for. First Thessalonians 5:18 (right after we are instructed to pray without ceasing) says, "In everything give thanks; for this is the will of God in Christ Jesus." Get that? It is God's will in Jesus that we give thanks for *everything*.
5. Do remain faithful to God in whatever testing we experience. James 1:2 says, "Count it all joy when you fall into various trials." Count it *all* joy.

God's prescription for us in handling closed doors is: WTPO— wait, trust, pray, obey.

CHAPTER 12

Taking Out the Cat Box for Jesus

Have you ever gone to work knowing in advance that what you were going to be called upon to do that day had the potential to bore you to death? Or have you ever had a job where for one reason or other you just dreaded going to work? Well, I have. And that is no way to live. When I had that particular job, I had not yet latched onto the principle we are going to consider here. Once the "lightbulb came on over my head" on this, I have never been bored again.

The principle to which I refer is found in Ephesians 6:5–9: "Bondservants be obedient to those who are your masters according to the flesh, with fear and trembling, in sincerity of heart, as to Christ; not with eye service as men pleasers, but as bondservants of Christ, doing the will of God from the heart with goodwill, DOING SERVICE UNTO THE LORD AND NOT TO MEN, knowing that whatever good anyone does, he will receive the same from the Lord, whether he is a slave or free." I supplied the capital letters in that one phrase because those words are the key to this study.

So what's up with being bondservants? Well, of course, the Bible must be interpreted with word usage of the time in which it was written. We don't have bondservants anymore. Or do we? During all those thirty-one years I was the chief weather anchor at WFAA-TV I was, strictly speaking, a bondservant. I always worked under contracts that I had signed, obligating me to work for a certain period of time for a certain amount of money. I was bound by the terms of those contracts. Fortunately the TV station was also bound by the contract terms. But you get the idea.

The point here is that we are to do what our bosses (or masters, in Bible terminology) tell us to do. And we are not to do it as "men pleasers." That is generic, of course. For many of my years at WFAA-TV, my bosses (or masters) were women. So we are not to be working to please the men or women over us. Well, then, who are we supposed to be pleasing? The passage says we are to be bondservants to Christ. And what will please Him in the way we do our work? He will be pleased if we do our work in the will of God from the heart and with goodwill.

The centerpiece of the passage is the next phrase, the one I did in all caps. We are to do our work unto the Lord and not to men. We are actually working for God. And the passage tells us we are to do it in goodwill. This goes to the principle in 2 Corinthians 9:7, the verse your pastor pulls out on "Stewardship Sunday," the plea for increased financial giving. It goes like this, "So let each one give as he purposes in his heart, not grudgingly or of necessity; for God loves a cheerful giver."

I propose to you that this verse is not only talking about our money, but also our time and effort. If we give our money, our time, and our effort with a cheerful attitude, God will be pleased. This passage says He loves such a person. This covers everything we do in life, even down to taking out the cat box. The original title of this study was "Taking Out the Cat Poop for Jesus." I decided that was a little too graphic for a title line. But I use it here in the text because it is exactly what I mean. *Whatever* we do, we can indeed do it as to the Lord, and He will be glorified.

I am certainly not the first person to come up with this idea. You may have heard of a little book called *The Practice of the Presence of God*. It was written by a seventeenth century Monk called Brother Lawrence. The book was actually compiled after his death from notes he had left regarding his life in a monastery. Brother Lawrence was assigned to the kitchen. His long work days consisted of cooking for the other monks and washing their dishes. It was a hot, steamy, wet, tedious job. But Brother Lawrence "got it." For him even the most mundane and unpleasant task could be a medium of God's love. Brother Lawrence was not doing these tasks to please men. He was doing them as unto God.

Now looking back at our Ephesians 6 passage, in verse 8 the word *whatever* sneaks up on us. It is not used in the way we often use it when getting a directive from a superior at work. You know, when the boss hands back to you a completed project with all kinds of reasons that it must redone. As soon as the door closes behind him or her, you might very well say, "Whatever!"

No, here it literally means whatever we do. That is to say that everything we do, we are to do with goodwill (cheerfulness), not just because the boss said so, but because it is a service to the Lord our God. Charles Haddon Spurgeon, the famous nineteenth century British theologian and preacher, had this to say on the subject: "The affairs of common life are the place to prove God's truth and bring Him glory."

How can doing common, mundane tasks bring God glory? In doing them, we Christian believers are God's representatives.

Do you think of yourself that way? Well, we are. As Christian believers, we are representing Jesus every day in our lives. The question is: Are we representing Him well? Or are we representing Him poorly? Unbelievers are observing us. Are they likely to say, "Wow! I want what he/she has?" Or not?

One more nugget from Ephesians 6:8. Don't miss it. Notice it says, "Whatever good anyone does, he will receive the same from the Lord." To what does that refer? Rewards! My Bible study notes take us to Colossians 3:23–25 in connection to this verse: "And whatever you do, do it heartily as to the Lord, knowing that from the Lord you will receive of the inheritance; for you serve the Lord Christ." Paul is speaking here of rewards in eternity. It tells us that *all* our works that we do as unto the Lord will be rewarded in eternity. Sounds good to me!

Now we are not talking about salvation here, of course. That is God's free gift to us. We cannot earn it. As Acts 16:31 says, "Believe in the Lord Jesus Christ and you will be saved." That's it. That's all, period. That will bring you into heaven when you leave this life. But once you get to heaven, eternal rewards are not equal. The more we do our earthly tasks, no matter how mundane, as unto the Lord, the more eternal rewards God will give us in heaven.

Well, that's it. I need to go take out the cat box now. Just kidding. Our last cat died several years ago. But every time I took that box outside I thought about this passage and did it unto the Lord. What a blessing!

CHAPTER 13

Communion Is Jewish?

Actually, yes it is. What we Christians call the Last Supper was in fact a Passover seder (meal). But it and all Passover seders before and since are loaded with Christian Messianic symbols.

Some years ago, dear Jewish friends of ours were kind enough to invite us to share their family seder on the first night of Passover. Of course, we were honored to accept. We had already talked to them about Yeshua (Jesus) being the Messiah. And I had told them of the connections between their Passover seder and communion. So, since we were to share that evening with them, I asked if I could show them those connections. I was very pleased that they said yes.

There is a strict formula for a Passover seder, a script you might say. It is punctuated by readings from the book of Exodus and foods representing various aspects of Jewish life during the time they were in bondage in Egypt and their deliverance by God at the initial Passover. That night God's angel of death literally passed over the houses of the Jews. They had received instructions from God to splash the blood of a sacrificed animal above their doorways. The Egyptians, of course, did not do this, and the angel of death took their firstborn sons. This set in motion the chain of events through which God delivered the Jews out of Egypt.

So that evening at our friends' house, we went through their traditional rituals at dinner. Then it was my turn …

I took them back to a point in the seder called the *Afikomen*. In Hebrew the word *afikomen* means "the one who has arrived." The *Afikomen* involves three pieces of unleavened bread (*matzoh*). The one who is presiding breaks the middle piece of this bread, wraps it in linen, and hides it. Later in the meal he brings it back. That is exactly what our friend had done at our dinner. And this ceremony, part of the commemoration of the Jews' deliverance from Egypt, had already been in place for around fifteen hundred years before that night in Jerusalem when Jesus had His last meal with His disciples.

On that night in Jerusalem two thousand or so years ago, Jesus was presiding at the seder. He performed the *Afikomen* ritual. Note the Christian symbolism present in this ancient Jewish tradition. The three pieces of bread represent to us the Godhead, the Trinity—the Father, the Son, and the Holy Spirit. The middle piece represents the Son, Jesus. It is broken, wrapped in linen, hidden, and later brought back, referring to His death, burial, and resurrection.

But on that Last Supper night, Jesus put a whole new twist on the *Afikomen*. When He brought back the middle piece of *matzoh*, which He had broken earlier in the meal, He broke it into more pieces and distributed it to His disciples around the table. He told them (and us by extension), "Take, eat. This is my body, broken for you. Do this in remembrance of Me." And that is exactly what we do now whenever we have communion in church. We are following a directive that Jesus instituted that night. That change in the Jewish ritual was huge. But wait …

Then Jesus instituted a second radical change in procedure.

Following the *Afikomen* came the third of what would normally be at least four cups of wine served during the seder. Jesus took this third cup of wine and passed it among His disciples at the table. Jews would recognize this was really a departure from ritual. They did not use their own cups. They all drank from this one cup, which Jesus passed around. But that's not all. The cup that Jesus passed around was special. The Greek says He picked up "the" cup," not "a" cup, but "*the*" cup. This has really special significance. Biblical scholars take this to mean that He used what is called at seder "Elijah's Cup." Nobody ever drank from that cup. It was filled with wine and set on the table. But it was reserved for Elijah. Old Testament prophecy said that Elijah was coming back. That cup was for Elijah, just in case he showed up at dinner.

Jews still pour Elijah's Cup at Passover seders. Our friends did it that night. But of course nobody drank from it.

When Jesus used Elijah's Cup, He was telling the disciples (and us by extension) that they were no longer to wait for Elijah. They were really waiting for the Messiah. And the wait was over. He was telling them Messiah is here now. And you are looking at Him. Then He said to the disciples, "This cup is the New Covenant in My blood. Do this as often as you do it in remembrance of Me." And of course we do this today in our Christian churches, just as Jesus instructed.

Then Jesus made one more startling change in procedure. He abruptly ended the seder. Normally there would have been at least one more cup of wine, more readings, and the main food courses.

But instead, Jesus stood up and said, "I will not drink again from the fruit of the vine until I drink it with you in My Father's Kingdom." Then, He led the disciples out into the night singing. They were probably singing what is called the Great Hillel. This consists of Psalms 115–118.
They are the traditional Psalms of deliverance that traditionally end a Passover seder.

They all went up to the Mount of Olives, where Jesus was betrayed. After several mock trials, He was crucified and buried. But three days later He rose from the grave so that those of us who believe in Him can have eternal life.

I had finished my explanation.

Both of our friends' children asked for copies of my notes and took them to their rooms. Have they since become believers in Yeshua? No. Not as far as we know. We had previously talked to our friends, their parents, about Yeshua being the Messiah. The mom seemed as though she thought there really might be something to this. But she would not commit. The dad said, "We kinda believe the same. We kinda believe different." The mom's parents were there that night. Her dad said he had heard everything I presented before. That was just not what he believed.

Every time we have a relationship with Jewish folks, I always give them my Christian testimony, including why I would love for them to become believers in Yeshua. My reason for wanting that? I care for them. And I am concerned about their place in eternity. Have any of our Jewish friends and acquaintances become believers? No. At least not yet. My wife, Janet, gets discouraged at this. But I tell her that we are just to do what we are supposed to do. It is not like selling a car. We just give the sales talk. It is not up to us to close the deal. That is up to God. .

And one more thing. On another occasion, while having dinner with these same Jewish friends, the wife said to me, "Okay, let's just get something out on the table here. You believe that if we don't believe what you believe about Jesus being the Messiah, we are going to hell, right?" No pressure there, huh?

I told her this, "First, let me say that I love you like a sister, and I will always love you whether you believe in Jesus/Yeshua or not. And yes, I believe you will go to hell if you don't." She then said, "So now you are going to drop us like a hot rock, right?" Why did she say that? Because all of their previous Christian friends had done just that when it turned out they rejected Jesus's claim as Messiah. I was shocked. Folks, that is not what Christian love is all about! I assured her again that we would always love her and her family whether they came to belief in Yeshua or not.

Now this Passover seder with our friends was some years ago. Their daughter and son were in their early teens. They are both well grown now and living in another city. We are still close friends with the parents. We still love their family. We always will. We Christians are supposed to love others, not "drop them like a hot rock." What kind of Christian testimony is that?

Do I still pray every day that these dear friends will come to believe in Yeshua the Messiah? You bet I do.

And I don't get discouraged because, as that great theologianYogi Berra once said, "It ain't over till it's over."

CHAPTER 14

Broadway Show Tickets

So, there was this couple in New York who received in the mail two tickets to a popular Broadway show. But there was no note or card telling them who sent the tickets. Of course they wondered who would do such a nice thing for them. But after thinking it over for a while, they figured it must be some good friend who for some reason wanted to be anonymous. Or maybe it was just a random act of kindness from someone. And they were tickets to a good Broadway show!

Well, the couple did go to this show on the designated evening, and they really enjoyed it. It was just as good as they thought it would be. The only thing was, when they got home that night, their house had been robbed. The robbers had made an investment. They bought and sent the couple the show tickets. And knowing what night this house would be empty, they took everything of value from it.

Our lives can be like this. While we are watching the "Broadway show" of worldly life around us, Satan and his minions are ransacking our lives. What we often see as glory is not true glory, the glory of God. It is false glory, the glory of the world, fool's gold.

Let's look at some places in the Bible where we see God's true glory. How about Psalm 19:1. The heavens declare the glory of God and the firmament shows His handiwork. What is the firmament? It is the sky or the heavens. In fact the Hebrew word for firmament can be translated as heaven. The sky and the heavens are great examples of God's glory. He created them.

The Hawaiian island of Maui is one of my favorite places. There is an old Hawaiian saying describing the island: Maui no ka oi. It means Maui is the best. I agree with that. I am thinking of a T-shirt I saw there at one of the many shops in the old whaling town of Lahaina. The writing on the front of the shirt said,

Maui Rules

1. Never judge a day by the weather.
2. The best things in life aren't things.

That is pretty profound, especially for a T-shirt. If you walk around Maui with your "antenna up" looking for God's glory, you will see mountains, ocean, whales, beaches, and unspeakable beauty. The best things in life aren't things. That means the best things in life are not possessions. They are God's glorious creations, which we are privileged to witness and enjoy.

Another manifestation of God's glory is found in Exodus 33:18–23. Here Moses asked God to show him His glory. God told him He would do that, but Moses could not see His face. That glory would be too much for a human. God told Moses that no human could see His face and live. So God prepared a cleft in the rock on the mountainside, put Moses in there and covered him with His hand as He passed by. Then God moved His hand and let Moses get a glimpse of His back.

After that God gave Moses the Ten Commandments. In the next chapter, Exodus 34, when Moses came down from the mountain with the stone tablets bearing the Ten Commandments, he did not realize that his face had a super-brilliant glow after being in God's presence. His face was so bright that the Israelites could not look directly at him. After that, Moses would put a veil over his face when he came back down to the people after conversing with God on the mountain. Now *that* is glory!

Paul spoke of this in 2 Corinthians 3:7. He says there that the people could not look at Moses because of the "glory of his face which was passing away." After a while, when God's glory had faded from Moses's face, the Israelites could look at him again. There is a nugget here for us. The longer we are away from God, the more His glory fades in us. This is certainly true in spiritual terms. But you can even think of it in literal terms. As we go through our lives as Christians, we may not think about it, but people are always observing us—looking at us, even when we are unaware of it. If we are operating within God's plan for our lives, people observing us will be able to see the radiance of God's glory in us.

It is our responsibility to exhibit that Christian radiance that will make those observing us say, "I want some of what he/she has!" Think about this, and you will realize I am right. Think of people that you know or have just seen who have such a radiance. You really can see it.

But if we as Christians are *not* reflecting God's glory in our lives, we are really blowing it. Not only are we out of God's plan in our own lives, but unbelievers who know us to be Christians are going to see the contradictions in our lives and be totally turned off at the thought of becoming a Christian. I really don't want somebody looking at me and saying, "Whoa, if that is what being a Christian looks like, you can keep it!"

And radiating God's glory is a continuing action. In John 7:37–38, at the Feast of the Tabernacles in Jerusalem, Jesus cried out to the crowd, "If anyone thirsts, let him come and drink. He who believes in Me, as the Scripture has said, out of his heart will flow rivers of living water." Rivers continue to run and run and run.

Another thing about the word *drink* in verse 37. This word is in the aorist tense in Greek. It denotes a continuing action. Jesus is saying keep on coming to Me, and the rivers of living water will keep on flowing out of you. We need to stay close to Jesus and not let His glory fade in us. We can keep those rivers of living water flowing in us if we regularly pray, read the Bible, meditate on it, get good Bible teaching, and practice assembling with other believers to encourage and be encouraged.

Paul says in Philippians 3:10 his goal is that he may "know Him (Christ) and the power of His resurrection, and the fellowship of His suffering, being conformed to His death, if by any means I am to attain resurrection from the dead." We cannot skip over that line about the fellowship of Christ's suffering. Fellowship means sharing. Christ suffered. Sometimes we Christians are going to have times of suffering. But take comfort in what God told Paul in 2 Corinthians 12:9 when Paul asked Him three times to remove the "thorn in the flesh" that was causing him suffering. God said he was not going to do that, but He told Paul, "My grace is sufficient for you." And His grace is sufficient for us too. That is a promise to claim. God makes a promise. He keeps it!

Jesus says in John 8:12, "I am the light of the world. He who follows Me shall not walk in darkness, but have the light of life." We can reflect that glorious light if we follow Jesus day by day, moment by moment. We cannot let ourselves be distracted by the passing "Broadway show" of worldly life.

CHAPTER 15

He Was Never in a Hurry

How do we spend our time? Are we always rushing from one place to another? Are we constantly flitting from one thing to another? Are we always trying to meet one deadline or another? That is pretty much the way it is in the world today. There are so many things competing for our attention. And there seems to be so little time to get them done. We consider time a very valuable commodity.

But look at any Bible passage about Jesus when He was here on earth, and you will find that He was never in a hurry. He always had a purpose. He always had a plan. They were actually the purposes and plans of God the Father. And Jesus was certain that His Father would accomplish both His purposes and plans through Him. But Jesus had something we often lack—patience.

Jesus was never irritated by delays or interruptions. In John 4 He patiently talked to the Samaritan woman at the well. And what happened there? Many people in her village came to belief in Him that day. His disciples were restless and wanted Him to move on. But Jesus stayed in that Samaritan village for two more days. And

John 4:41 says, "Many more believed because of His own word." The rest of His schedule could wait.

And in John chapter 11, when Jesus received word from Mary and Martha that their brother Lazarus was gravely ill, once again He stayed two days in the place where He was. Only then did He go to Bethany, where Mary, Martha, and Lazarus lived. These three were among Jesus's closest friends on earth. But He didn't drop everything and rush off to Bethany. He knew what he was doing and when to do it. When He got to Bethany, He raised Lazarus from the dead.

And then there was the time in Mark chapter 5 when a ruler of the synagogue came to Jesus with an urgent plea to come to his house and heal his dying daughter. Verse 24 says, "So Jesus went with him, and a great multitude followed Him and thronged Him." Remember what happened next? One of the people in that crowd was a woman who had been experiencing a bleeding problem for twelve years. She had such faith in Jesus that she said in verse 28, "If only I may touch His clothes, I shall be made well."

She did touch the hem of His garment, and immediately she was healed. Jesus stopped and patiently talked to her, commending her on her great faith. Verse 35 says, "While He was still speaking to her, some came from the ruler of the synagogue's house and said, your daughter is dead, why trouble the teacher any further?" But in verse 36 Jesus said to the ruler of the synagogue, "Do not be afraid, only believe." He then went to the house of the ruler of the synagogue and revived the man's daughter. Once again, He was not in a hurry. And He was willing to be interrupted in what He was doing. And once again He accomplished His Father's purpose and plan.

This reminds me of a one panel cartoon I saw a few years ago. In the scene a man wearing a black suit and a white clerical collar is kneeling in an office with a number of bookshelves all around. He is obviously praying. His wife is coming through the door. She says, "Oh good, you're not doing anything important." I reminded my own wife of that cartoon several times when I was holed up in my office writing these studies. Both the man in the cartoon and I *were* doing something important. But I told my wife that she could feel free to interrupt me any time. Jesus is the model. She didn't interrupt me often, but when she did, it was okay. I was able to regain focus and keep writing.

In these three New Testament stories, Jesus kept His focus during delays and interruptions. Well, okay, He was and is God. And I certainly am not. Neither are you. So how can we go about keeping our focus on God's plan for us? We must follow the instructions of the apostle Paul in Ephesians 5:15: "See then that you walk circumspectly, not as fools, but as wise, redeeming the time because the days are evil."

To walk circumspectly means to be cautious, prudent, watchful on all sides, carefully examining all circumstances that may affect our actions. The study notes in my Bible relating to this passage say that it means in this context to step gingerly, watching our paths so as to avoid contact with undesirable influences.

When we face a delay or an interruption, we must just ask God to make His will our will and leave the details to Him. Whatever the situation, we are to give it to God. Don't waste time worrying about how we are going to catch up. This does not absolve us from the responsibility of completing assigned tasks. But as Christian believers we must realize that if God is not in control of our lives, whatever we might accomplish through our own efforts doesn't amount to a hill of beans anyway.

Put another way, we must make ourselves available to God. When we do that, He can and will use us. He will take our natural gifts and add His touch of Divine creativity and, through the power of the Holy Spirit, accomplish things through us that we could never imagine. When you tell God, "Okay, I am ready to do whatever You want me to do," you will be amazed that you will actually receive the ability to do it. Take, for instance, talking to people about Jesus. Whether in public speaking or one on one personal contact, once you start doing it, you will find that you actually enjoy it. God *will* use you if you truly surrender yourself to Him.

But, meanwhile, Satan and his demons are not just sitting around twiddling their thumbs. When they observe you serving God, they are going to try to get you to implement another plan in your life—their Satanic plan. If we are distracted by negative, self-defeating or impure thoughts, we are neutralized in God's plan. We are taken out of action. So how are we to avoid stepping into Satan's traps? How can we make sure our delays or interruptions are not leading us toward evil? Well, let's revisit that instruction to walk circumspectly.

Colossians 3:2: "Set your mind in things above, and not things of the earth."
Second Corinthians 10:5: "Bringing every thought into captivity to the obedience of Christ."
Colossians 3:16: "Let the Word of Christ dwell in you richly in all wisdom, teaching and admonishing one another in psalms and hymns and spiritual songs, singing with grace in your hearts to the Lord."
Philippians 4:8: "Finally brethren, whatever things are true, whatever things are noble, whatever things are just, whatever things are pure, whatever things are lovely, whatever things are of good report, if there is any virtue, and if there is anything praiseworthy, meditate on these things."

If we maintain the mind-set expressed in these passages, then we can handle delays or interruptions, just as Christ did. We will be able to discern if the delays or interruptions are leading us to evil. If they are, we can avoid them. If they are not, we can deal with them and then continue "redeeming the time." He was never in a hurry. We don't have to be either.

Philippians 4:13 is our power source: "I can do all things through Christ who strengthens me."

CHAPTER 16

A Can of Worms?

Let's talk about spiritual gifts.

If you are a Christian believer, you have at least one spiritual gift. It is your responsibility to discover it and use it. Most of us are rather lax in this. I only discovered my primary spiritual gift *after* I began to use it regularly. That seems a bit backward doesn't it? Well, as it turns out, after I began doing these Bible studies at WFAA-TV, regular attendees of the studies told me that I was encouraging them. My primary gift is encouragement. Who knew? But why did I title this particular study as I did? We'll get to that. Stay with me.

First of all, what are spiritual gifts? They are extraordinary abilities that the Holy Spirit gives individual people when they accept Jesus Christ as their personal Savior. See I Corinthians 12:1, 4–11, and 28.

Verse 1: "Now, concerning spiritual gifts, brethren, I do not want you to be ignorant." Verses 4–12: "There are diversities of gifts, but the same Spirit. There are differences of ministries, but the same Lord. And there are diversities of activities, but it is the same God who works all in all. But the manifestation of the Spirit is given to each one for profit of all: for to one is given the word of wisdom through the Spirit, to another the word of knowledge through the same Spirit, to another faith by the same Spirit, to another gifts of healings by the same Spirit, to another the working of miracles, to another prophecy, to another discerning of spirits, to another different kinds of tongues, to another interpretation of tongues. But one in the same Spirit works all these things, distributing to each one individually as He wills." And verse 28: "And God has appointed these in the church: first apostles, second prophets, third teachers, after that miracles, then gifts of healings, helps, administration, varieties of tongues."

Also see Romans 12:6–8: "Having then gifts differing according to the grace that is given to us, let us use them: If prophecy, let us prophesy in proportion to our faith; or ministry, let us use it in our ministering; he who teaches, in teaching; he who exhorts, in exhortation; he who gives, with liberality; he who leads, with diligence; he who shows mercy, with cheerfulness."

And then, Ephesians 4:11–12 "And He Himself gave some to be apostles, some prophets, some evangelists, some pastors and teachers."

And finally 1 Peter 4:10–11: "As each one has received a gift, minister it to one another, as good stewards of the manifold grace of God. If anyone speaks, let him speak as the oracles of God. If anyone ministers, let him do it with the ability which God supplies, that in all things God may be glorified through Jesus Christ, to whom belong glory and dominion forever and ever, amen."

Now, whenever these passages mention "the Spirit" notice that the word *Spirit* begins with a capital letter. This, of course, refers to the Holy Spirit. And you may have also noticed that in using these gifts "he" is to do this, that, and the other. No use of the word *she*? Nope, the *he* is generic. You females didn't think God would leave you ungifted, did you? Well, He did not. Every Christian, male or female, has at least one of these gifts.

And you may have been looking over these lists and wondering where I came up with the realization that my personal spiritual gift is encouragement. That specific word is not found in the listings. But, in Romans 12:8 notice the word *exhortation*. That means encouragement. To exhort means to encourage. The Hebrews 10:24–25 passage uses it as well: "And let us consider one another in order to stir up love and good works, not forsaking the assembling of ourselves together as is the manner of some, but exhorting one another, and so much the more as you see the Day approaching."

So there you are. Encouragement is a spiritual gift. And I am grateful that it is mine.

Time out for a moment. Before we move on, let me point out an important sidebar to our study here. Look at the instruction in the middle of this Hebrews 10 passage. We Christians are not to forsake assembling together. Do you realize what that means? We are supposed to go to church regularly! Hey, it's in the Bible. We need to be doing it.

Okay, back to encouragement. Some of the other gifts are tangential to encouragement. *Helps* in 1 Corinthians 12:28 means coming alongside a believer who has a need. Maybe it's a ride to a doctor's appointment or just putting your arm around the shoulder of someone at the right time. The gift of mercies is also related to encouragement. It could be physical or spiritual support. And all the gifts, of course, spring out of God's grace.

71

Well, enough about me. Now, *you* should carefully consider for yourself all the gifts in these lists. Look at the gifts. Ask yourself, "What do I see here that I am good at? Am I doing it? Should I be doing it?" You have at least one of these gifts, maybe more. You need to put it (or them) to use. I regret that it took me so long to discover mine. But it is never too late, as long as you are breathing!

Okay, time to open the "Can of Worms." And most of you know where I am going with this. There is disagreement among Christians today on the current validity of four of these spiritual gifts. They are the gifts of healings, miracles, speaking in tongues, and the interpretation of tongues. A majority of Christian churches today believe that these four gifts were phased out as the New Testament was completed and put into its final form.

But some Christian churches believe that these gifts are still in place. These are notably churches called Pentecostal, Nazarene, and Charismatic. Who is right about this? Well, guess what. We don't have to go there. We don't have to decide. It is not our job to judge other Christians, whether we are on the one side of this issue or the other.

I love what my friend Dr. Larry Poland says about this. Larry was raised in a very conservative Midwestern Christian home and church. After high school he went away to Wheaton College in Illinois. Well, Wheaton has a pretty conservative Christian atmosphere. But Larry became friends with another student there who came from a Pentecostal background. That sent up a red flag to Larry. But Larry says he soon came to realize that this young man didn't roll around on the floor and do crazy things. He just loved Jesus!

We Christians should look for ways to emphasize our unity, not our differences. We can disagree on the continuing validity of these four gifts of healings, miracles, tongues, and interpretation of tongues. We just need to focus on Jesus Christ and cut each other some slack in how we worship Him.

Put away the can opener.

CHAPTER 17

Be Careful; This Plate Is Very Hot!

How many times have we heard a restaurant server say that when delivering food to our table? Be careful, this plate is very hot! And, of course, our natural tendency is to touch the plate, in spite of the warning. That's human nature. Well, let's expand this thought past hot plates in a restaurant. Consider Proverbs 6:27–29: "Can a man take fire to his bosom and his clothes not be burned? Can one walk on hot coals and his feet not be seared? So is he who goes into his neighbor's wife. Whoever touches her shall not be innocent."

This is in the Old Testament, of course. But Jesus also addressed this subject in Matthew 5:28, in His Sermon on the Mount. And talk about expanding a principle! Jesus said here, "But, I say to you, whoever looks at woman to lust for her has already committed adultery in his heart." Well, we are not going to get too hung up on adultery here (although it will come up again in this study). It is a sin with very serious consequences. But for our purposes, it is just an example of yielding to *any* temptation to go outside God's established boundaries.

Our human nature wants to test God's boundaries, to see what happens when we go outside them. This tendency had an early beginning in the Garden of Eden. Eve yielded to Satan's temptation, ate the forbidden fruit, and then shared it with Adam. Satan told them nothing bad would happen to them. Wrong!

Even if we don't step over God's boundaries, we often try negotiating with God over them. How close to the edge do we want to live? Do we have to have a total understanding of God's reason for establishing boundaries? No, we don't. God sets rules. We are to follow those rules or face consequences.

Look at Deuteronomy 1:26–28: "Behold, I set before you a blessing and a curse: the blessing if you obey the commandments of the Lord your God, which I command you today; and the curse if you do not obey the commandments of the Lord your God." That is pretty clear. God knows how to do curses. We do not want to go there!

We humans are all subject to hungering, longing, yearning, thirsting, or in the old cowboy vernacular, hankering for something. We are all subject to *desire* for the fruit of the forbidden tree. King David desired Bathsheba. (Here comes adultery again.) He clearly understood God's boundaries. But his desire was so strong that he stepped right over them to satisfy his desire. Bathsheba was certainly not blameless here. But since she was a subject of the king, she had little or no choice in the matter. But they both suffered the consequences of the sin they committed.

There is a key question we have to ask ourselves when we are faced with temptation to step outside God's boundaries. Joseph asked it in Genesis 39:9. He was in charge of the house of Potiphar, captain of the Egyptian Pharaoh's guard. Potiphar's wife made sexual advances to the young, handsome Joseph. But Joseph asked himself this key question: "How then can I do this great wickedness and sin against God?" That was Joseph's view of life. That viewpoint prepared him to say no to temptation.

No is the essential word when it comes to temptation. It is not a sin to be tempted. We all face temptations. The sin is giving in to the temptation. All potential sin has a starting point. At that point we have the choice to yield to temptation or to refuse it. Our ability to resist and refuse temptation is directly related to our relationship, or lack of relationship, with God.

If we go through life focused on ourselves, our succumbing to temptations is inevitable. Temptation whispers seductively to us that sin will satisfy our desires. No one else will know about it. It will be okay. In fact it will be fine. But, of course, it is not okay. It is not fine. Somebody does see it. And that somebody is God Himself. He sees *everything*. There is no hiding from Him.

If, however, we go through life focused on the fact that we belong to God and are committed to reflecting His glory in the things we do, we will be much more likely in the face of temptation to just say no.

None of us likes to be manipulated, right? We don't like to be used by someone else. Well, that is what happens when we yield to temptation. Satan or one of his demon minions is manipulating us, using us. Temptation is a primary tool of the Devil.

And there is another aspect to yielding to temptation. It is not only a personal sin of our own. It is opening the doorway to cause somebody else to sin. To use two cases we have already considered here, Eve caused Adam to sin. King David caused Bathsheba to sin. Jesus said in Matthew 18:6–7, "Whoever causes one of these little ones who believe in Me to sin, it would be better for him if a millstone were hung around his neck and he were drowned in the depths of the sea." Wow! That's a pretty strong warning about causing someone else to sin!

We might say, "Well at least I don't do that." But are we sure we don't cause others to sin? What about times when we are unforgiving? Our lack of forgiveness can cause the other party to be unforgiving as well. Two sins for the price of one! Satan loves it! Or what if someone observes us venting anger and copies our actions? What if we engage in telling dirty jokes, encouraging the listener to sin by laughing at them? (This is the "coarse jesting" about which we are warned in Ephesians 5:4.) What about drawing others into "little white lies"? As if there were such a thing. All lies are black as coal. And then there is gossip. We have many ways of sinning and drawing others into the sin with us. When we do all these things, we are doing Satan's job for him. I often think that Satan has plenty of opportunities just to take the day off. We can manufacture our own temptations without his urging.

Whatever we do, day by day, minute by minute, we need to be aware of all these warnings about yielding to temptations:

1. Consider the consequences of a sin before we do it.
2. Whenever we do blow it, turn immediately to God to confess the sin. We will still face the consequences. But with confession God will restore us to fellowship with Him, so that we can move on.
3. Surrender to God's ways. Stay within His boundaries.

The reason He established boundaries for us? So that we will not get burned.

Be careful, the sin plate is very hot!

CHAPTER 18

God's School of Obedience—A Five-Step Program

I'm sure we can all agree that being obedient to God is a good thing. But nobody said it would be easy. So here are five steps that will lead us on the path to obedience.

Step One Is Trust
Here we go to my favorite Old Testament Bible verses. Proverbs 3:5–6: "Trust in the Lord with all your heart and lean not on your own understanding. In all your ways acknowledge Him and He shall direct your paths." That's the Bible quote. But Eugene Peterson's paraphrase in his book *The Message* might be helpful here. It says, "Trust God from the bottom of your heart. Don't try to figure out everything on your own. Listen for God's voice in everything you do, everywhere you go. He's the one who will keep you on track."

Faith in God through our relationship with Jesus Christ must be the basis for trust. You can't trust somebody in whom you do not have complete faith. So, first of all, we have to believe God is who He says He is (in the Bible)—the almighty, all knowing, omnipresent, unchanging, gracious, loving ruler of the universe. Then, having faith in Him, we must trust His plans, His methods, and His timing. We can deepen our level of trust in Him by listening for His instructions in our lives. Then we can reach obedience. God delights in blessing those who trust and obey Him. There is an old hymn that expresses this point very well. It says, "Trust and obey, for there's no other way to be happy in Jesus, but to trust and obey."

Step Two Is Waiting

This means waiting for God's timing. Having patience is a very challenging thing for us humans. When we don't know what to do, we often make our next move based on our own limited understanding, hoping that God will approve and bless the action. That is truly putting the cart before the horse (Bet you haven't heard that expression in a long time). God is more than willing to show us what to do. Proverbs 3:6 clearly says that He will direct our paths (*if* we trust Him to do so). And He has given us the Holy Spirit as a guide (John 14:16–17). Jesus says, "And I will pray the Father and He will give you another Helper, that He may abide with you forever—The Spirit of truth, whom the world cannot receive, because it neither sees Him nor knows Him; but you know Him, for He dwells with you and will be in you." We just have to wait with an attitude of trust until we are certain we have directions from God as to what path to take.

Step Three Is Meditating

While we are waiting, we are to meditate. Hey, that sounds spiritual. But what does it really mean? Well, if you know how to worry (And who doesn't?), you know how to meditate. You take an issue and roll it over and over again in your mind. What's the difference? When you worry, you fret over an issue and become more and more upset the more you go over it in your mind. When you meditate, you roll an issue over and over in your mind with the idea of seeking God's solution. The Bible often tells us that He will take care of business for us, if we will just stop trying to do things in our own power (which is nonexistent) and our own understanding (which is way limited). Just surrender our will to Him! Here we go back to Proverbs 3:5. But there is also more to meditation. We also need to pray and read the Bible during this process. God can use any portion of the Bible to guide us. Even if you read a passage that seems to you to have nothing to do with your issue at hand, if you persevere in reading, you will gain knowledge and wisdom. What is the difference between the two? Knowledge is something you learn. Wisdom is knowing how to apply it.

Step Four Is Listening

We need to listen to the quiet prompting of the Holy Spirit. He doesn't shout. He generally whispers. He might speak to you through your Bible reading, through something your pastor says in a sermon, or something your Sunday school teacher says in a lesson. Those are pretty obvious. But the Holy Spirit can also speak to you through something your spouse says, something the checkout person at the supermarket or even McDonalds says, *or even* something you just overhear someone say when that someone is not even speaking to you. He may speak to you just through a restless feeling you have, or a seemingly random thought that comes into your head. If you keep your "spiritual antenna" up at all times, you will be amazed at things the Holy Spirit says to you.

Step Five Is Walking

Even though the way ahead of you is not totally clear, if you feel God nudging you in some direction, walk in that direction. God doesn't tell us everything at once. Hebrews 11:8 talks about Abraham as an example of faith in action. God told him to get up and go. He got up and went. He went, not knowing where he was going, just because God told him to do so. We can and should obey God without totally or even partially understanding what He has in mind for us. The theological term for this is progressive revelation. He deals with us on a need to know basis. If He told us everything about our lives, the weight of that knowledge would crush us. My favorite nonbiblical example of this is in the 1992 movie *A Few Good Men*. Jack Nicholson's marine colonel character shouts at the court-martial officers, "The truth? You don't want the truth! You can't handle the truth!" That is actually a really good illustration of progressive revelation. If God revealed everything to us, we would not need faith. And God does require us to have faith as part of our obedience.

Trust, wait, meditate, listen, and walk.

CHAPTER 19

Chariots of Fire

This is the name of a 1981 movie based on a true story about two British runners in the 1924 Olympics. One was Jewish. One was Christian. It is a very entertaining film. And it is still available at amazon.com and iTunes as of this writing. If you haven't seen it you should, because not only is it entertaining, it is a story about faith, hope, character, and grace.

Harold Abrams was the Jewish fellow in the story. He was an outstanding athlete, strongly motivated by overcoming anti-Semitism. The Christian runner was Scotsman Eric Liddell (pronounced Ly' dul), who runs for the glory of God. That's a pretty good start for a movie, don't you think? But there's a lot more to their interwoven stories.

Perhaps you already know that the title of this film, *Chariots of Fire*, is taken from the Bible. And it is part of a great story too. The biblical story concerns the Old Testament prophet Elisha. In the days of ancient Israel, whenever God's people, Israel, got off track in their walk with Him, He would raise up a prophet to set them straight. This happened over and over again through a long period of Old Testament history. Some of these prophets you have no doubt heard of, or even studied: Isaiah, Elijah, and Jeremiah, to name a few. Elisha doesn't get quite as much "press" as the first three. And there were others as well. But, let's focus on Elisha. Elisha figures prominently in several stories. But the one we go to here occurred sometime between 850 and 800 BC.

The nation of Israel had divided into two kingdoms shortly after Solomon's death. Israel was in the north, and Judah was in the south. Well, during the period noted just above, the Syrians were threatening to invade the northern kingdom, Israel. Somebody was always threatening Israel in those days. Come to think of it, somebody is always threatening Israel today! Seems things haven't changed much. But, I digress ...

Our story is found in 2 Kings 6:8–18. The king of Syria, Ben-Hadad, found out that someone was warning the Israelites about Syrian troop movements. The Syrian king thought there must be an Israelite spy in his camp. But actually God was revealing the information to Elisha, the Jewish prophet. Ben-Hadad discovered where Elisha was through his own (human) intelligence department. Elisha had been found in a city called Dothan, in the central highlands of Israel. So Ben-Hadad dispatched a large Syrian army, including many horses and chariots, to round up Elisha and bring him back to Syrian headquarters.

Elisha had a servant with him. One morning the servant got up early and went outside his tent. Much to his shock and chagrin, he saw that the city of Dothan was completely surrounded by the Syrian army with its multitudes of horses and chariots. The servant brought Elisha out to show him this overwhelming hostile military force. And he asked Elisha, "Alas, my master! What shall we do?"

Elisha told the servant, "Do not fear, for those who are with us are more than those who are with them." Then Elisha prayed and asked God to open the servant's (spiritual) eyes. The Lord did open the eyes of the young man, and "behold the mountain was full of horses and chariots of fire all around Elisha." When the Syrians came down to attack, Elisha prayed that God would strike them all with blindness. And God did just that. Elisha was delivered.

When we base our evaluation of our life situations on obvious circumstances instead of placing our faith in God, we struggle to move forward. We *must* realize that we are not self-sufficient. God alone can and will meet our needs. But often it takes our being brought down to a situation of apparent hopelessness for us to finally say to God, "I'm at the end of my rope. Help!"

This story is one of those times of apparent hopelessness. In spite of the presence of a huge hostile army bearing down on him, Elisha's faith in God was so strong that he keenly felt God's presence protecting him. He was calm and relaxed. His servant must have thought he was nuts. But he knew, and he asked God to reveal to the servant that they had divine backup. The Syrian army was no match for the angelic protection God had sent. Elisha gave himself over to that protection without hesitation.

We have to give ourselves over to God's divine protection in order to receive deliverance from God. This takes faith in God and admission of total inadequacy in ourselves. When I think about this story of Elisha and the chariots, I get goose bumps. Why? Because I believe this really happened. This is not just some sci-fi tale This is the Word of God. If we could only come up with the kind of faith Elisha had!

Paul had something to say about this kind of situation in 2 Corinthians 5:7: "For we walk by faith, not by sight." And back to the Old Testament, 1 Chronicles 16:11 says, "Seek the Lord and His strength. Seek His face evermore." *Evermore* here can also be translated *continually*. How do we seek the Lord and His face continually?

1. Read the Bible at least a little every day. The every day part is important.
2. Pray. Prayer is more than a wish list. Ask God for guidance. Meditate. Listen for Him to answer your prayers. And don't forget to praise Him, and bring Him your gratitude. Set aside a time to pray every day. And pray at other times as well. Prayers don't always have to be lengthy and all-encompassing.

If you believe in Christ as your Savior, God's chariots of fire are all around you.

I didn't tell you the plot details of the movie *Chariots of Fire*. Instead I urge you to watch it, and look for the principles of faith, hope, character, grace, and deliverance. I believe you will be entertained *and* blessed.

Hey, Watch Your Mouth!

We all have times when we say something, and as soon as it is out of our mouths we want it back. We know we shouldn't have said it. But now it is out there registering on the minds and in the hearts of everybody in earshot. Most of you folks reading this are likely Christians. This is especially important for us as believers, because the Bible has things to say directly to us about proper communications. And if there are some unbelievers (pre-Christians) among us here, the principles we are going to discuss in this study still apply to you too!

When I was doing these weekly Bible studies at WFAA-TV, the management let me use the main conference room. The only caveat was (and I proposed it) that if anybody needed the room for business purposes, we would find another room that day. But most Wednesdays at 1:00 p.m. the room was ours. This room was in the center of the building. The entrance was formed by two wide glass doors in a main hallway. Many of our coworkers would pass by and glance in during our times together.

I often reminded everybody, including myself, that all these passersby glancers-in knew what we were doing—having a Christian Bible study and prayer time. Consciously or not, they would be checking us out whenever they saw us or spoke with us outside that room. They were going to be evaluating our speech and conduct. Would we be walking the Christian walk outside of Bible study to back up our talking the talk in Bible study?

I often say, and you will see this more than once in this little book, that as Christian believers we represent Jesus in the world around us every day. The question is are we representing Him well? Or are we representing Him poorly? Our verbal communication is a huge part of that.

The apostle Paul has something to say on this subject in Ephesians 4:29–33: "Let no corrupt word proceed out of your mouth, but what is good for necessary edification, that it may impart grace to the hearers." That is verse 29. But it is only the first part of Paul's thought here. His use of the word *corrupt* might need a little amplification. In context it means speech that is degrading, with unsound principles or poor moral values. Not only is such speech inappropriate to those around us, it also grieves the Holy Spirit. The passage goes on. Verse 30 then says, "And do not grieve the Holy Spirit of God, by Whom you were sealed for the day of redemption."

And Paul is not done with us yet. Verses 31–33 say, "Let all bitterness, wrath, anger, clamor and evil speaking be put away from you (along) with all malice. And be kind to one another, tenderhearted, forgiving one another, even as God in Christ forgave you."

The study notes in my Bible regarding these verses suggest to us that if we take care to remember that the Holy Spirit lives in us

Christians, we will be more selective about what we think, read, watch, do, and say. Doing or saying any of the things Paul tells us to avoid in these verses reveals shallowness in a Christian's commitment to God.

And Paul is not ready to let us up yet. In chapter 5, after giving us the positive instruction to walk in love as Christ also loved us and sacrificed Himself for us, he has some specific warnings against things that are not fitting for the saints. Who are the saints here? He is not talking about Saint Francis of Assisi or Saint John Paul II. In New Testament parlance, *saints* refers to Christian believers—you and me. These instructions are for *us*.

In verses and 4, Paul tells us, "But fornication and all uncleanness or covetousness let not even be named among you as fitting for the saints (us); neither filthiness, nor foolish talking, nor coarse jesting, but rather of thanks." *Filthiness, foolish talking*, and *coarse jesting*. Think on those words when you are tempted to share an off-color remark or dirty joke. We are just not supposed to go there. These are specific prohibitions for Christian believers!

But, let's put the shoe on the other foot. Suppose you find yourself in a situation where somebody else tells a dirty joke in your presence. What is your response? I knew a pastor in Detroit many years ago who said that while he was getting a haircut, his barber started to tell him a dirty joke. The pastor pointed to his own ear and said, "Does this look like a garbage can?" That was effective in stopping the joke, of course, but this pastor said that he realized later it was not a very gracious way to handle the situation.

So what should you do? Try to move away? Not always possible. Laugh nervously? No, that is an endorsement. You might hold up a hand and politely say, "I have a feeling I don't want to hear the end of this story." That's not bad. But I have come up with a response that really works for me. I have passed it along to others, and several people have told me it works for them. When the person finishes with the joke, I just say "Ouch!" What have I done? I have expressed disapproval in a nonjudgmental way. I have found that when I have done this, the person who told the dirty joke has never done so again in my presence.

But let's get back to the Bible for some reenforcing principles on proper speech. King David wrote in Psalm 19:14: "Let the words of my mouth and the meditation of my heart be acceptable in Your sight, O Lord, my strength and my Redeemer."

Colossians 3:16 says, "Let the Word of Christ dwell in you richly in all wisdom, teaching and admonishing one another in Psalms and hymns and spiritual songs, singing with grace in your hearts to the Lord."

What did people say about the way Jesus spoke? Luke 4:22: "So all bore witness to Him and marveled at the gracious words which proceeded out of His mouth."

Then, to wrap up, let's go to Philippians 4:8, where Paul tells the believers in the church at Philippi (and us by extension), "Finally brethren, whatever things are true, whatever things are noble, whatever things are just, whatever things are pure, whatever things are lovely, whatever things are of good report, if there is any virtue and if there is anything praiseworthy—meditate on these things."

Hey, Christian believer! Watch your mouth!

CHAPTER 21

Is Life Really Like a Box of Chocolates?

Forrest Gump thought so. Remember that wonderful Tom Hanks film from 1994? His character, Forrest Gump, sat on a park bench with a box of chocolates. He told the person next to him that his mother had taught him, "Life is like a box of chocolates. You never know what you are going to get." Good thought. But I would like to place a little different perspective on the box of chocolates.

Like Forrest Gump, when you open a box of chocolates, you carefully consider the contents, trying to decide which piece to select. Truly you don't know what you are going to get until finally you take a piece and make a small, experimental bite—you know, just a little piece off the side, near the bottom. And don't tell me you haven't done that. Lying is a sin, you know! Then, if the piece is not what you expected or something that is not to your taste, you surreptitiously put it back in the box when you think no one is looking. And you select another piece—or two or three.

The point is that it is what's inside that piece of chocolate that counts. So it seems to me a better phrase would be: Life is like a box of chocolates. It's what's inside that counts.

Christian believer, what is inside of *you*? In 2 Timothy 1:7, Paul says, "For God has not given us a spirit of fear, but of power and of love and of a sound mind." Now those are the things that *should* be inside of us as Christians. God has certainly made them available to us, *if* we will take advantage of them. What do I mean by that? Well, don't accuse me of "bait and switch" here, but the secret to spirituality is not *what* is inside you, but *who*. And, of course, I refer here to the Holy Spirit.

God wants to be close to us, so close in fact, that He makes Himself available to us believers on a 24/7 basis. It is what is theologically called the indwelling of the Holy Spirit. The Holy Spirit is actually inside you if you are a Christian believer.

In John 14:16–18, Jesus says, "And I will pray the Father, and He will give you another Helper, that He may abide with you forever— The Spirit of truth, whom the world cannot receive, because it neither sees Him nor knows Him. but you know Him, for He dwells with you and will be in you." Did you notice that all three members of the Trinity are involved in these verses? Jesus the Son prays to God the Father regarding the Holy Spirit.

Jesus talks more about the coming of the Helper in John 15:26: "But when the Helper comes, whom I shall send to you from the Father, the Spirit of truth Who proceeds from the Father, He will testify of Me, and you also will bear witness, because you have been with Me from the beginning." And also in John 16:12–13, Jesus says, "I still have many things to tell you, but you cannot hear them now. However, when He, the Spirit of truth has come, He will guide you into all truth; for He will not speak on His own authority, but whatever He hears (from God the Father), He will speak."

Why did Jesus tell His disciples here that He had many more things to tell them, but they could not hear them at that point? Jesus had told these guys everything their human understanding could absorb at that point. And in fact, they didn't even understand all of what Jesus had already told them. But certainly to understand the further things God would reveal to them, they would need the Holy Spirit to guide them. And they would not receive the indwelling of the Holy Spirit until Jesus had been crucified and resurrected. He was to leave the Holy Spirit in His place when He went back to heaven.

We Christian believers, of course, are indwelled by the Holy Spirit the moment we believe in Christ. But we must choose to follow His guidance if we are to understand and use the spiritual things God wants us to know and do. The Holy Spirit is God's power source for us. He is there inside us. But we have to plug into Him to receive guidance. We have to stop trying to get through life on our own power. That is futile and delusional. We have no power.

And here's another thing about the Holy Spirit. All the help and guidance we can get from Him is found in the Bible. He will guide us in understanding the Bible and applying what we learn from it. But do you see the catch here? The Holy Spirit cannot guide us in understanding and applying the Bible *unless we first read it*. He cannot explain something to us that we have not read and studied.

Now, of course, Satan and his demon minions are not going to be just sitting around twiddling their thumbs while we plug into the divine Holy Spirit power source. They will do their best to distract us and discourage us. But take heart. John 4:4b says, "He who is within you is greater than he who is in the world." That first He uses a capital *H* referring to God. The second is a lowercase *h* referring to Satan. Our power source is greater than Satan. We just have to stay plugged in. (Okay, I know that the original Greek text didn't use caps and lowercase letters. But they are used in the translation here. And I believe that this English language Bible is still the divinely inspired word of God. Caps and lowercase are valid usage.)

So what are some of the ways that the Holy Spirit makes His power available to us?

Galatians 5:22–23: "But the fruit of the Spirit is love, joy, peace, longsuffering, kindness, goodness, faithfulness, gentleness, self control." His power enables us to manifest these things in our lives.

Romans 8:26: "Likewise the (Holy) Spirit helps us in our weakness. For we do not know what we should pray for as we ought. But the Spirit Himself makes intercession for us with groanings which cannot be uttered." When we don't know what to pray, if we call on Him, He will intercede for us in our prayers in ways that cannot be expressed in human language.

Acts 9:31. The Holy Spirit provides peace, edification and comfort.

Romans 8:16. The Holy Spirit identifies Christians as sons (children) of God.

He makes it possible for us to exhibit His spiritual fruits. He intercedes for us. He testifies for us. He's got our back.

Think of the Holy Spirit like this. Say you are good friends with Arnold Schwarzenegger. (Okay, I wrote this in 2002. Plug in some other big, strong guy of this era if you like.) So, you and Arnold are strolling along Rodeo Drive in Beverly Hills, just having a nice chat. You stop for a moment to look in the window at Hugo Boss or Chanel. You turn around and … Who is the meanest movie villain you can think of? Well, he is walking toward you in a very menacing manner. Just at that point, Arnold comes back into view, puts his arm around your shoulder and says to the bad guy, "He's with me." That's the Holy Spirit. He's got you covered *if* you call on him.

The Holy Spirit doesn't compel you to walk in God's path for your life. You can walk down the street with Satan if you like. That's your choice. A lot of folks do that. But there are consequences. I think of Proverbs 27:12: "A prudent man foresees evil and hides himself. The simple pass on and are punished." What you and I should be doing is keeping our spiritual antennae tuned, listening for that quiet voice of the Holy Spirit saying to us, "This is the way. Walk in it." He is there for us 24/7. We just have to plug in.

It's who's inside that counts.

CHAPTER 22

God's Résumé Shows He's Overqualified!

Read Ephesians 3:1–21.

If somebody came to your door and told you he could solve all your problems, would you believe him? Well ... no. Before you placed your trust in him you would want to learn about who and what he is. You would want to see his résumé. Actually you would really want and need to develop a personal relationship with this person before you put your trust in him. The word *him* here is generic. After this, I am going with *him*. You may plug in *her* if you like.

You certainly want to verify the qualifications of the person who does your taxes or handles your investments. You want to thoroughly check out a doctor before letting him do surgery on you. I had a total right knee replacement in 2011. You can be sure that beforehand I checked out the surgeon who was going to do it. And by the way, he is really good. If you need a new knee or hip, give me a shout, I am happy to recommend him.

Since I retired from the TV weather business, I have represented a number of clients, endorsing them in television and radio advertisements. I always do a thorough evaluation of the quality of their goods or services before I put my name on their brands. And, yes, there have been a few prospective clients whom I have declined to represent. All these things come under the term due diligence. One really needs to pursue due diligence before making any important decision. One's career, financial security, health, or even life can depend on it.

But most folks don't do the most important due diligence of all. Have you done your due diligence on God? Or do you blindly make prayer requests of God without ever making an effort to find out who He is and what qualifications He has. A lot of people lift up immediate pressing needs to Him because they have heard Him referred to as God. They figure that means He is powerful. But they don't really want to pursue getting to know who He actually is, much less develop a personal relationship with Him. And that's too bad, because such people are really missing out on what our God truly has to offer us.

When you read a person's résumé you get a feel for what he has accomplished and what he can do to help your company or you personally. So with that in mind, I propose that in order to know God and develop a trusting relationship with Him, you definitely need to read His résumé. What? God has a résumé? You bet He does. It is called the Bible. Okay, you saw that one coming. But it is true. The Bible really is God's résumé. Reading it is the only way to familiarize yourself with His background, characteristics, and, for want of a better word, His skills. What is God good at?

As I said at first, you have to get to know somebody before you can trust him. The better you know that person, the more you know just how much you can trust him. And wouldn't it be great to be able to fully trust God? Well, in Ephesians 3:1–21, Paul helps us with an understanding of God and all that He is able to do for us.

This passage deals with what is called the Mystery Doctrine. The "mystery" has to do with Jesus Christ and God's gift of grace to humanity. Why is it called the Mystery Doctrine? Paul uses the word *mystery* in chapter 3, verses 4 and 9 because, although the Old Testament is full of messianic prophecies, the exact manifestation of these prophecies was not fully revealed until Paul proclaimed in this passage the identity of the Messiah as Jesus Christ.

In the New Testament, Jesus arrived on earth and fulfilled *all* three-hundred-plus Old Testament prophecies. But even then not everybody "got it." Most of the Jews missed out because they had their own ideas of what this Messiah would look like. They were expecting an all-powerful military leader who would overthrow Roman control in Palestine and set up an earthly kingdom. Well, they got way ahead of themselves. Jesus will eventually come back as a conquering military Deliverer. But God doesn't always do things the way humans want. In fact He seldom does. Pick up your Bible and look at Isaiah 55:8–9.

Most of the Jews at the time when Jesus was on earth didn't recognize Him as the Messiah. Oh, and guess what. Most Jews today don't either. They are still waiting for their Messiah, not realizing that He came to earth almost two thousand years ago. And He came on the exact day prophesied by Daniel more than five hundred years earlier! That prophecy is in Daniel chapters 9 and 10. And, yes, you need a theologian or true Bible scholar to explain the details. That is not me. But theologians and true Bible scholars have it figured out. And it is true. Daniel made a *really* accurate "five-hundred-year forecast." TV weather people have trouble telling what is going to occur in the next seven days.

But back to Ephesians 3. Paul is writing here to gentiles. So, what is a gentile? Well, anybody who is not a Jew is a gentile (Hebrew word *goy*). Paul's ministry to the gentiles in this passage reminds us that, although the Jews are God's chosen people, God's offer of eternal salvation is open to anybody, Jew *or* gentile. Paul's principle ministry was to gentiles, whereas Peter and Jesus's other original disciples ministered principally to Jews. In fact the first eight thousand or so "Christians" were Jews. I use quotation marks around the word Christian because the positive use of that word wasn't really used to describe followers of Jesus until much later. In Greek it means "little Christ" and was at first a demeaning term used by people who did not believe in Jesus.

In verses 9 and 10 here, Paul talks about clearing up this mystery by revealing that God is going to accomplish all His eternal purposes through Jesus Christ. Then in the rest of chapter 3, Paul tells us about the relationship that he has developed with God through Jesus, and that we all have the opportunity to develop that same relationship.

In verse 16, he says that God will "grant you (us), according to the riches of His glory, to be strengthened with might through His Spirit in the inner man." Then verses 17–19 tell us that if we have faith in Christ He will "dwell in your (our) hearts through faith that you (we), being rooted and grounded in love, may be able to comprehend with all the saints (believers) what is the width and length and depth and height—to know the love of Christ which passes knowledge; that you (we) may be filled with all the goodness of God."

Notice the word *comprehend* in verse 18. That means we will able to understand all these things. If we have faith in Christ, God can give us an understanding of supernatural things. And what is the extent of the things God can do in our lives? Matthew 19:26b says, "With God, all things are possible." Jesus said this. He is reminding us that God is limited by nothing—not tragedy, not fear, not sin, not even death. Jesus came back from death. And you will too if you have put your faith in Him!

But if we remain handicapped by limited knowledge of God, if we don't learn about Him through the Bible, we will tend to try to limit Him, ascribing human traits to Him. We will say things such as, "How can God possibly get me out of this mess I have gotten myself into?" If we have that attitude, guess what. We are going to remain hopelessly stuck in whatever mess we are embroiled. The Bible continually reveals to us (*if* we read and study it) that God is greater than any person, power, or circumstance. Nothing surprises God. Nothing is overwhelming to Him.

Some years ago at WFAA-TV, I was tasked with hiring a new meteorologist for our staff. I found this fellow named Steve McCauley who was working at a station in Amarillo. When I looked over his résumé I told him, "You are overqualified for this job. But if that doesn't bother you, it doesn't bother me." Of course I am not comparing Steve McCauley to God. But you get the human application.

God is *way* overqualified to handle *anything* in our lives. Look at Ephesians 3:20: "Now to Him (God) who is able to do exceedingly abundantly above all we ask or think, according to the power that works in us, to Him (God) be glory in the church by Christ Jesus, to all generations, forever and ever. Amen."

All I can say to that is, "Thank You, Lord!"

And another "Amen."

CHAPTER 23

I'm Sorry ... This Is a Recording

Most of us might as well add that second phrase whenever we apologize to a family member, friend, or coworker for something we have said or done. We often use a word or expression so much that it loses all meaning. "I'm sorry" can be just a very short, perfunctory, conciliatory sentence mumbled in a shallow effort to restore a positive relationship with an offended party.

I remember when I was a kid, my dad once told me he was going to make a sign saying "I'm sorry" and hang it around my neck. Then, every time I did something wrong, I could just point to the sign and save us both time and conversation. I hadn't thought about that episode from my childhood in many years until I ran across the passage in Scripture that is the inspiration for this study. More about that passage in a moment.

Back to my childhood first. I don't remember being all that bad. But then, we need to try to see ourselves as others see us. My dad was not a harsh person. In fact he was a wonderful, loving father. I have great memories of him. He was just "calling them as he saw them." I had frustrated him in some way. And there really is validity to the phrase, "Perception is reality." Our self-perception means nothing to others. They form their perception of us by their observation of our behavior in their presence.

This goes back to my frequently expressed thought in these studies that people are always watching us. If we are known to be Christians, we have targets on our own backs. People will be watching us, especially when we are unaware, to see how well our behavior represents Jesus. Are we walking the walk or just talking the talk?

Now about that passage in Scripture. It is in 2 Corinthians 7.8–12: (Paul writing to the believers in the church at Corinth) "For even if I made you sorry with my letter (possibly 1 Corinthians or maybe another letter that was not preserved), I do not regret it. Though I did regret it. For I perceive that the same epistle made you sorry, though only for a while. Now, I rejoice that you were made sorry, but that your sorrow lead to repentance. For you were made sorry in a godly manner, that you might suffer loss from us in nothing. For godly sorrow produces repentance leading to salvation, not to be regretted; but the sorrow of the world produces death. For observe this very thing, that you sorrowed in a godly manner: What diligence it produced in you, what clearing of yourselves, what indignation, what fear, what vehement desire, what zeal, what vindication! In all things you proved yourselves to be clear in this matter. Therefore, although I wrote to you, I did not do it for the sake of him who had done the wrong, nor for the sake of him who had suffered the wrong, but that our care for you in the sight of God might appear to you."

Whew! When I read Paul's writings in the New Testament, I generally say, "Paul, couldn't you have simplified this a little?" But fortunately the Holy Spirit can help us understand whatever we read in the Bible, *if* we ask Him for His help. In fact I suggest that you do ask the Holy Spirit for a clear understanding of this passage right now, and then read it again. That is what I did.

In this brief passage, Paul uses the word *sorry* four times, the word *sorrow* three times, and the word *sorrowed* once. But the key is another word that he uses in verse 9 and again in verse 10: *repentance.* "Your sorrow lead to repentance" is in verse 9. And, "Godly sorrow produces repentance" is in verse 10. This tells us that if we are *truly* sorry for something we have said or done to someone, then we will be convicted to have a change of mind, heart, and attitude about it. That is godly sorrow.

Paul indicates in this passage that this convicting sorrow was what the Corinthian believers experienced after receiving what he refers to as "my letter" (which had preceded 2 Corinthians). In that previous letter, Paul had "called out" the Corinthian believers for sins and abuses that were going on in that church body, stemming from the presence of false teachers in Corinth. In showing them what they needed to do, he had gotten on their case in a pretty strong manner. They had expressed some sorrow. But it was superficial. Note verse 8, where Paul says they were, "sorry, but only for a while."

Note also in verse 8; referring to that previous letter, he first regretted being so tough on them, but now he is glad he sent it, because they "got it." They understood the adjustment they needed to make in their lives, and they made that adjustment—repentance.

So what exactly is repentance? I have touched on it a couple of times here. But the Greek word used here for repentance simply means to change—to change your mind, attitude, and heart about something. As an example, when we repent of any sin, we simply agree with God that what we have been doing is wrong. But when we do "repent," we must then seek God's help in that change of mind, attitude, and heart, or we will fall right back into whatever sin pattern it was from which we repented.

So when we find ourselves saying, "I'm sorry" to someone, we need to stop and think. Am I truly expressing sorrow and a change of mind, attitude, and heart? Am I truly making a confession of sin? Or am I just making conversation? There is a huge difference. And that, of course, is the point of this study.

But before we end here, I need to point out something in verse 10 of our passage that could cause confusion. Notice Paul says, "For Godly sorrow produces repentance leading to salvation." Paul is speaking to believers here. Aren't they already saved, whether or not they have godly sorrow for wrongs they have done? Yes, they are. The word *salvation* in the New Testament does not always refer to being rescued from hell. The word for that is *justification*. That happens when you believe in Christ. God forgives your sins and "justifies" you as righteous. You will be going to heaven when you die. You are "saved" at that point. You have "salvation." But salvation is an ongoing process.

The word for salvation Paul uses here in verse 10 refers to that process, which is really *sanctification*. It means to set apart. Expressing godly sorrow is a manifestation of that concept. It is turning away from sin, setting ourselves apart from the world, and getting back into fellowship with God. As Christians, when we sin, we break that fellowship. Sin estranges us from God. It neutralizes our witness. When we repent of a sin, as in expressing true godly sorrow over something we have done or said, we restore our fellowship with God and thus restore our Christian witness.

There is one more use for the word *salvation* in the New Testament. But it speaks of our future as Christians and does not apply to our passage. It refers to what happens when we die. That is the final part of the salvation process. It is called *glorification*. This is our status in heaven after we die (or after the Rapture). This is being glorified in the presence of Christ in heaven.

God desires to mold us and shape us in His image. Isaiah 64:8 says, "We are the clay and You are our potter." When we repent of our sins and are in fellowship with God, He can spin that potter's wheel and start shaping us into what He wants to make us by His almighty power and in His divine will.

In heaven, nobody will ever have to say, "I'm sorry." Revelation 21:4 tells us that there will be, "No more death, nor sorrow nor crying." But until we get there, when we say "I'm sorry," let's be sure we really mean it!

CHAPTER 24

The Guy with the Technicolor Dream Coat

The account of the life of Joseph in Genesis chapters 37–50 is such a good story that Andrew Lloyd Webber and Tim Rice turned it into a hit musical show on the stages of London and New York. The title comes, of course, from the coat or tunic that Joseph's father Jacob made for him when he was a teenager. My Bible calls the garment a "tunic of many colors." Many translations say "coat of many colors." The word *coat* has come to be traditional. The Hebrew phrase may simply mean that it had long sleeves. But it was likely of some distinctive color or design. And it was probably very costly.

Lloyd Webber and Rice took the concept and ran with it. They called their show, *Joseph and the Amazing Technicolor Dream Coat.* That's show biz for you! And amazingly, Lloyd Webber and Rice were teenagers themselves when they wrote the show. It was a school project. And it was their first collaboration. Both went on to illustrious careers in musical theater, at first together and later separately. Andrew Lloyd Webber wrote the music for his shows. Tim Rice was the lyricist.

I have never seen or read anything to indicate where either one of these guys is spiritually. But this show is very true to the Bible. It is still produced occasionally. And at the time of this writing a DVD of the show is still available at amazon.com. It stars a then rather young Donny Osmond as Joseph. I highly recommend you see it if you get a chance.

So, what is the story of Joseph about? Well, it is a story about God's will. And not only that, the story illustrates that God's will is in three parts: His decreed will, His desired will, and His permissive will. God's decreed will is eventually going to happen. If He decrees something, nothing will be able to keep it from happening in the end. But along the way God does cut mankind some slack, actually a lot of slack. We shall see this as we go along.

So is this "Technicolor dream coat" just a hook to get your attention? No, it was actually rather important in the story. But it was really more of a "nightmare coat" for Joseph. He was the next youngest of twelve brothers in Jacob's household. But he was his father's favorite. This caused his brothers to be jealous of him. In fact chapter 37 verse 4 says, "they hated him and could not speak peaceably to him." And Joseph didn't help himself much with them. Read on.

Joseph had a God-given gift of being able to interpret dreams. In verses 5 through 10 in chapter 37, he tells his father and his brothers about two dreams he has had. One is about sheaves of corn. The other is about the moon and the stars. In Joseph's interpretation of both these dreams, he says that his parents and brothers will be bowing down to him—Joseph. Now the brothers were really steamed. Little did they know at the time that Joseph's interpretation of these dreams actually revealed the *decreed* will of God. This was going to happen eventually, and nothing or nobody could stop it.

There are many other examples of God's decreed will in the Bible. Here are a couple. Daniel 4:35 says that no one can ward off God's hand. In Isaiah 46:10, God says that He will establish His purpose. He will accomplish all His good pleasure. And, of course, in both (and all such) cases, these things do happen.

Now what about God's *desired* will? This is what He desires for each of us to do. It involves our discovering His plan and staying in it in our lives. God issues commands in Scripture—the Ten Commandments, for example. Any such commandment expresses what God desires us to do. Honor you father and mother, put no other God's before Me, don't murder, etc. (Exodus 20:1–17). And in the New Testament, for example in Ephesians 5:25 where husbands are commanded to love their wives. God wants us to do these things. He desires that we do them, But do we always obey His commands? Well, you know that we don't.

Joseph's brothers certainly *tried* not to do God's desired will. They came up with a plan to kill Joseph. Then they would never have to bow down to him. He would be forever out of the picture. Not so fast, brothers. This is where God's permissive will comes in. God permits sinful people to do whatever evil is in their hearts. But guess what. He even uses such things to accomplish His plan.

This principle is continued as Joseph's story goes on in Genesis 39. The brothers took Joseph out in the desert and planned to throw him in a deep pit where he would die. But just then along came a caravan of traders, and they decided it would be better to sell Joseph to them as a slave. So that's what they did. Then they killed an animal and put its blood on Joseph's colorful coat. They took the bloody coat home with them and showed it to their father, Jacob. They told him that a wild animal had killed Joseph.

Meanwhile the traders took Joseph to Egypt and sold him to a guy named Potiphar, who was the captain of pharaoh's elite guard. Bad, right? Well, not really. Joseph was such a good slave that Potiphar trusted him enough to put him in charge of his household. Good, right? Well, not really. Potiphar's wife tried to seduce this handsome young slave. He refused and ran away, saying to her, "How then can I do this great wickedness and sin against God?" Potiphar's wife grabbed Joseph's garment as he escaped and showed it to the husband, telling him that it was Joseph who had actually tried to seduce her. Potiphar had Joseph thrown in prison. And when you got thrown into that prison in Egypt, you were there to stay. Bad, right? Well, not exactly. Joseph was such a model prisoner that he was made chief trustee of the prison. He was pretty much running the place. Better, but he was still in prison.

Then in Genesis 40–41, while in prison, Joseph interpreted more dreams, first for two fellow prisoners and eventually for pharaoh himself. He interpreted pharaoh's dreams to predict seven years of plenty followed seven years of famine. Pharaoh believed Joseph's interpretations and put him in charge of the whole country. He became pharaoh's prime minister. As such, he arranged bountiful harvests during the years of plenty and administered grain storage and distribution during the years of famine.

Well, meanwhile back in Joseph's homeland, famine had also struck hard. And Jacob's family was running out of food. So Jacob sent his eleven remaining sons to Egypt to buy food. When they get there, they bowed down to the prime minister, not having a clue that he was their long-lost brother. God's decreed will was accomplished. And Joseph and his family were reunited.

This, of course is a *really* condensed story of Joseph's life. You really should pick up your Bible and read it, looking for the examples of God's decreed, desired, and permissive will.

Did Joseph and his family live happily ever after in Egypt? Not exactly. After Joseph's death, a new pharaoh took over Egypt and enslaved the descendants of Jacob's family because they were becoming too numerous. This pharaoh felt they were a threat. But that evil also accomplished God's plan. By the way, God had changed Jacob's name to Israel. So that's why from this point on in the Bible we hear of the "children of Israel." Sounds like a good name for a country—Israel!

The time of slavery in Egypt kept the Israelites from intermarrying with pagans. This kept their strain pure for their later conquest of the land God had promised Abraham so long ago, earlier in Genesis. God has things figured out—big time!

So the overall picture in the story of Joseph is that God's permissive will we can thwart. But He will use whatever we do for His purposes. God's desired will we can disobey, but there will be consequences. And eventually God's decreed will is accomplished no matter what.

What are our takeaways from the story of Joseph?

1. It is obviously better for us to be in God's will than out of it. So we need to pray that His will for us will be made clear to us and get on board.
2. We should always put our hope and confidence in God. Read the Bible and pray for understanding it. The Holy Spirit will help you there.

3. Don't be discouraged when things are not going well in your life. Look at Joseph. He persevered through unbelievable difficulties.

In the show *Joseph and the Amazing Technicolor Dream Coat*, when Joseph has been thrown in the Egyptian prison, the narrator tells him not to be discouraged. She says, "We've read the book, and you come out on top." The book? The Bible.

One more note: The Israelites considered Joseph so important to their heritage that they kept his bones for hundreds of years— through Egyptian slavery and the wanderings in the wilderness. When they finally took possession of the Promised Land, they buried his bones there. Without Joseph, there would have been no Jewish nation.

CHAPTER 25

You Want Me to Do What?

God has plans for each of us. He has things for us to do. And He tells us these things. The problem is that often we are not listening when God is speaking to us. And that's a major problem. Certainly we cannot carry out God's instructions if we don't know what they are. The importance of listening to God is a subject that comes up often in these studies. But even when we do pick up on God's instructions to us, we always want to know more than He is going to tell us. We would like a phone call or an e-mail from God outlining His whole itinerary for us. Guess what. That ain't happening!

God has this annoying habit of giving us our marching orders on a need to know basis. We will never get His whole plan at once. He knows it would overwhelm us. So we are supposed to act on the instructions we *do* get. And we can do this *if* we have faith that further divine instructions will be coming forth in His timing. One of the best examples of this kind of faith is found in Genesis 12:1–5.

The Lord told Abram, "Get out of your country from your family and from your father's house, to a land that I will show you. I will make you a great nation; I will bless you and make your name great. And you shall be a blessing. I will bless those who bless you, and I will curse him who curses you. And in you all the families of the earth will be blessed."

Before we proceed here, a little back story is necessary. This guy Abram was descended from Noah, through Noah's son Shem (whose name is the root of the word Semite or Semitic). Abram was living in his dad's house (well, okay, a compound of tents more than likely) with his wife Sarai and other family members in a place called Ur of the Chaldees. Many Bible scholars take this to be a city of that name that was located on the Tigris River about fifty miles or so from the point at which the Tigris and Euphrates join before emptying into the Persian Gulf.

In Genesis 11:31 we see Abram's father, Terah, leaving Ur, taking his whole family, including Abram and Sarai and his grandson Lot, and moving them all to a place called Haran. There Abram's father died. Biblical historians tell us that Haran was likely the Assyrian name for a city called Hurrian, the ruins of which are in modern-day Turkey.

So where did God direct Abram and company to move? He directed them to a land called Canaan. He told them to settle there. Not only that, God promised Abram that this land would belong to his descendants. This is the first mention of Canaan in the Bible. And where was Canaan? Well, Canaan corresponds to modern-day Israel, Palestine, Lebanon, western Jordan, and southwestern Syria. Hmm, interesting. God promised all that real estate to Abram's descendants. But more about that later.

In Genesis 12:1–5, God gave Abram a direct order: "Get out of your country from your family." As usual, God did not give out the whole plan. All Abram got from God here were two things:

one, move, and two, "I am going to make you a great nation." That's it.

Now, this is where Abram might well have said to God, "You want me to do what? I'm seventy-five years old. Sarai and I have been married a long time. She's barren. We have no kids. We are both way beyond child-making and childbearing years. We just moved. My dad just died. I have my whole family to look after, yada, yada, yada." Well, Abram could have said that. But he didn't. What *did* he do? He saluted God smartly and said, "Yes, sir, let's do this!" Abram had faith that God would give him further instructions as necessary.

And that is what we are supposed to do when we sense God telling us to do something that is not in our comfort zone, indeed something that does not make sense to us. But that's not what we usually do, is it? We are inclined to ask God questions similar to the ones Abram could have asked but didn't. Abram's faith example to us says not to worry about details; just get up and *do* whatever God tells us to do. We are to have faith in God *and* act on that faith.

Moving over to the New Testament, check out Hebrews 11:8, which says, "By faith Abraham obeyed when he was called to go out to the place which he would receive as an inheritance, and he went out, not knowing where he was going." Of course, this is the same person as Abram. In Genesis 17, God had changed Abram's name to Abraham and changed Sarai's name to Sarah.

We may not know where we are going in life. But rest assured that if God calls us out to do something in faith, He will be right there with us every step of the way, revealing to us our next step and the next and so on. Now the first step in that journey of faith is belief in Jesus Christ. Jesus Himself said in John 14:6, "I am the way the truth and the light. No man comes to the Father except through Me."

And in Acts 16:31, Paul told the Philippian jailer, "Believe on the Lord Jesus Christ and you will be saved, you and your household." (The jailer and all his family placed their trust in Christ). God's plan is pretty simple really—believe in Jesus as your personal savior and wait for further instructions. Those instructions will be forthcoming in God's timing. Proverbs 3:5–6 tell us, "Trust in the Lord with all your heart and lean not on your own understanding. In all your ways acknowledge Him and He shall direct your paths." Step by step by step. And that is the main point of this study.

But there is a lot going on in Genesis 12:1–5. And I would be remiss if I didn't point out one other principle this brief passage contains. Note that in verse 2 God told Abraham he would make him a great nation. And in verse 3 He tells Abraham, "I will bless those who bless you and curse him who curses you." Who is the *you* here? It is the great nation that God plans to make of Abraham. This nation will be made up of Abraham's, then Isaac's, and then Jacob's descendants. Then in verse 7 God tells Abraham that He is giving the land of Canaan to them. Who are the descendants of Abraham, Isaac, and Jacob? They are the people who would become known first as Israelites and then as Jews. The modern-day Jewish state of Israel makes up a small part of the Promised Land of Canaan. God is saying here that eventually the Jews will own all of Canaan—Israel, Palestine, Lebanon, western Jordan, and southwestern Syria.

Now back to verse 3, where God says He will, "bless those who bless you (the Jewish people) and curse him who curses you (the Jewish people). God does not look with favor on anti-Semitism. We in America would do well to remember this. If we bless our ally Israel, God will bless us. If we abandon Israel, He will curse us. I didn't make this up. It's in the Bible.

Psalm 122:6: "Pray for the peace of Jerusalem. May they prosper who love you."

CHAPTER 26

God's Big Wooden Mallet

The occasion was the day when I received the first paycheck in a new contract year at WFAA-TV. I got a nice raise, for which I was thankful, of course. My second order of business on that Friday morning was to revise my household accounts budget, working out how to distribute the proceeds of my raise, including giving to our church. But, my first order of business was to do my morning devotional readings and prayer time. That was indeed the proper order.

One of my readings that morning was Dr. Charles Stanley's daily devotional. The first four verses in the Scripture he used were Proverbs 3:7–10. Here's that passage:

7. Do not be wise in your own eyes;
    Fear the Lord and depart from evil.
8. It will be health to your flesh
    And strength to your bones.
9. Honor the Lord with your possessions
    And with the first fruits of all your increase;
10. So your barns will be filled with plenty,
    And your vats will overflow with new wine.

Wham! God isn't subtle. It made me think of those wonderful old Warner Brothers Looney Tunes cartoons featuring the likes of Bugs Bunny and Yosemite Sam, Tweety Bird and Sylvester the Cat, and my personal favorite, Foghorn Leghorn, whose nemesis was little Henry Hawk. Frequently Sam, Sylvester, and Foghorn would be on the receiving end of a large wooden mallet applied forcefully to the head. God has a big wooden mallet of His own. And He doesn't hesitate to use it.

Okay, I already had a conviction to increase my giving to our church. But what a strong and timely reminder verse 9 in this passage supplied. Our little church was struggling financially at that time. And one of the things on my daily prayer list was that God would reveal to all our church members, including me, what He wanted us to do about that. Be careful what you pray for, right?

Now, the funny part was that verse 9 was not the main focus of Dr. Stanley's devotional that day. In fact he did not deal directly with that verse. But there it was staring *me* in the face. "Honor the Lord with the first fruits of all your increase." God was clearly assigning priority for me. I was being instructed to consider first how much of that raise to allocate to our church. Every other category would come after that.

Well, I smiled to myself (I was alone at my desk), rolled my eyes, and said, "Okay, God, You got me again." I had already pretty much figured out what those "first fruits" would be, but God just whacked me over the head with His spiritual mallet to make sure He had my attention.

Now although the thrust of Dr. Stanley's devotion was not on giving, when you look at this passage as a whole, it all comes together.

Verses 7 and 8 in Proverbs 3 say, "Do not be wise in your own eyes. Fear the Lord and depart from evil. It will be health to your flesh and strength to your bones." Well, of course these verses lead up to the next verse on giving. Proverbs 1:7 tells us, "The fear of the Lord is the beginning of knowledge." But many translations use the word wisdom. If we do as instructed and "fear the Lord," we will not be tempted to be wise in our own eyes. We are to get our wisdom from God in discerning our level of giving (and everything else).

And what about that phrase "Fear the Lord"? That doesn't really mean to be afraid of Him—of what He might do to you if He disapproves of something you are doing. Rather, it means to consider with awe His attributes—His power, universality, truth, consistency, and wisdom, and His love. If we approach God in this manner, we will be able to make a commitment to go to Him for guidance in all areas of our lives.

Verse 8 tells us if we do this, it will be "health to our flesh and strength to our bones." This doesn't only mean physical health and strength. It represents spiritual health and strength, which are necessary for growth into spiritual maturity in our relationship with God through Jesus Christ.

Then, on the other side of verse 9, the giving verse, we find that verse 10 tells us what will happen if we do give the first fruits of our increase to God. Our barns will be full, and our vats will overflow with new wine. Does that mean if we give a lot to the church, God will make us rich? No. But it does mean that God will provide for His obedient children. He will provide us our needs. Our needs, not our wants. Our wants might not be what God knows to be our needs.

Then, alongside this passage, we might look at Matthew 6:19–21, where Jesus says, "Do not lay up for yourselves treasures on earth, where moth and rust destroy and where thieves break in and steal, but lay up for yourselves treasures in heaven, where neither moth nor rust destroy and where thieves do not break in and steal. For where your treasure is, there your heart will be also."

This does not mean we should refrain from saving money, making investments, or buying life insurance. After all, Proverbs 13:22 tells us, "A good man leaves an inheritance for his children's children." Money is not evil. That idea comes from a frequently misquoted Scripture. First Timothy 6:10 says, "For the LOVE of money is the root of all kinds of evil." I supplied the capital letters. But that is the point. Having or making money is fine as long as it does not become an idol. It is a matter of priority. God comes first, not money.

Now I have told you a couple of times here that giving was not the focus of Dr. Stanley's devotional that day. So what was the primary focus? It was on the next two verses in Proverbs 3—verses 11 and 12: "My son do not despise the chastening of the Lord, nor detest His correction. For whom the Lord loves He corrects, just as a father the son in whom he delights."

Well what do you know? It all ties in. Remember I said that our little church was struggling financially at this time? Well, God was telling us that we in that church were not doing quite what He had in mind. He could have let the church prosper. But first He wanted us to come to Him for guidance—for correction. We are not to be discouraged when God chastens us in some way. He only does that because He loves us and wants to nudge us back into His plan—to put us on the correct course.

To wrap up, we just go back to a couple of earlier verses in this rich chapter in Proverbs. Look at verses 5 and 6 in chapter 3. These have long been my life verses. They say, "Trust in the Lord with all your heart, and lean not on your own understanding. In all your ways acknowledge Him and He shall direct your paths."

Sometimes with a big wooden mallet …

CHAPTER 27

I'll See That You Win the Race!

In 1959 famous movie director Cecil B. DeMille made an epic film called *Ben-Hur*. The story was based on a book written by Civil War General Lew Wallace. The book and the movie both had the subtitle *A Tale of the Christ*. If you have never seen this movie, you should. As of the time I am writing this, it is still available for purchase or rental. DeMille chose Charlton Heston to play the title role of Ben-Hur. He had cast Heston three years previously as Moses in another epic, *The Ten Commandments*.

The climax of the movie *Ben-Hur* is a spectacular eleven-minute chariot race. Heston told DeMille he did not want to use a stuntman for this sequence. He had learned to drive a two-horse chariot for *The Ten Commandments*. But these racing chariots were pulled by four horses and were much more difficult to handle. Heston asked DeMille for permission to get the necessary training to drive a four-horse chariot. DeMille gave him an okay on his request. And so Heston did just that. Then, after demonstrating his newly acquired skill for the director, Heston told DeMille, "I can drive the chariot, but I don't know if I can drive it well enough to win the race." Without hesitation DeMille said, "You just keep driving the chariot. I'll see that you win the race."

And that is pretty much what Peter tells us in 1 Peter 1:3–6:

To wit, "Blessed be the God and Father of our Lord Jesus Christ, who according to His abundant mercy has begotten us again to a living hope through the resurrection of Jesus Christ from the dead, to an inheritance incorruptible and undefiled, that does not fade away, reserved in heaven for you, who are kept by the power of God through faith for salvation ready to be revealed in the last time. In this you greatly rejoice, though now, for a little while, if need be, you have been grieved by various trials."

Now *that* is some encouragement for us Christian believers.

First Peter has only five chapters. At only ten or eleven pages, it is a short and easy read. But it gives us instructions on "driving the chariot" and assures us that if we just drive it to the best of our ability, God will see us through any and all trials to victory.

God has things He wants us to do. But it is necessary for us to stop and look at what God Himself has done, what He is doing, and what He is going to do for us. Christianity is all about what God does. What we are to do is respond to His love for us. We, as Christians, are incredibly blessed to have a relationship with the almighty God of the universe through Jesus Christ. This relationship is not based on the merit of anything we do. It is all about God's grace to us.

Need encouragement? Need assurance? God offers us both of those things Big Time all through the Bible. I am reminded of a classic Christian hymn, "Blessed Assurance." The opening lines say, "Blessed assurance, Jesus is mine. Oh what a foretaste of glory

divine. Heir of salvation, purchase of God. Born of His Spirit, washed in His blood."
Sounds a lot like 1 Peter 1:3–6, doesn't it?

Let's go to some more biblical promises from God that encourage us by offering His blessed assurance.

Jeremiah 29:11 tells us, "For I know the thoughts that I think toward you, says the Lord, thoughts of peace and not of evil, to give you a future and a hope." You might be thinking, *Wait a minute. That's Old Testament. Wasn't God talking to His chosen people the Jews?* Yes, but He was speaking not only to the Jews, but to everybody everywhere. God made His salvation available to *all*. Everybody who believes in Jesus Christ as his or her personal Savior has God's blessed assurance.

Moving back to the New Testament, 2 Timothy 2:13 says, "If we are faithless, He (God) remains faithful. He cannot deny Himself." That is to say, God knows we are going to fail. As humans we are weak. God understands this. He knows we will experience doubt and discouragement. But He is faithful. Once we have believed in Christ we have—here it comes again—blessed assurance.

As Christians we have eternal security. In John 10:27–29, Jesus Himself says, "My sheep (believers) hear My voice, and I know them, and they follow Me. And I give them eternal life, and they shall never perish; neither shall anyone snatch them out of My hand. My Father, Who has given them to Me, is greater than all; and no one is able to snatch them out of My Father's hand. I and My Father are One." We should put that passage on the refrigerator where we will see it every day. Talk about encouragement! Talk about blessed assurance!

Then, in Philippians 4:19, Paul tells us that God will supply all our needs according to His riches in glory by Christ Jesus. Note that He will supply our needs, not our wants. God knows what we need. We often confuse what we need with what we want.

We must remember that God is in control. Problems, even tragedies, in our lives are no reason to bail out on God. That 1 Peter passage says that we will have trials. All the more reason to sit tight with our trust in God and faith in Christ when the going gets tough. Missionary Corrie Ten Boom said, "When the train goes into a tunnel and everything goes dark, do you jump off the train? No. You sit tight and trust the engineer to get you through the tunnel."

As Jeremiah told us at the beginning of this study, God has good plans for us, and He will give us hope and a future.

Just keep driving the chariot; God will see that you win the race.

CHAPTER 28

Drippy Christian Faucets

Read John chapter 7.

The setting at the beginning of this chapter is Galilee. Jesus and the disciples were hanging out there because He knew that the Pharisees and the Sadducees had begun to plot to kill Him if He showed up in Jerusalem. And it was not yet time for that to occur. The time of year (in the calendar we use) was late September or early October in the third year of Jesus's ministry on earth.

Many people had believed in Him as the Messiah. But many more had rejected Him, largely due to pressure put on them by these Pharisees and Sadducees—the leaders of the Jewish religious establishment. These two groups were strongly opposed to Jesus because He was a real threat to their positions of authority. It wasn't so much the Jewish people who were hostile to Jesus; it was their religious leaders.

In verses 1 through 9 we see that it was time for Jews to head for Jerusalem for the Feast of Sukkot (Tabernacles), one of the three great Jewish religious festivals held annually. During the Feast of the Tabernacles, people came to Jerusalem and lived in "booths" made from branches of trees for eight days. This feast commemorated the forty years the Jews had spent wandering in the desert. It also served as a feast of thanksgiving for the year's harvest.

The other two great annual festivals were Pesach (Passover), celebrating the Jews' deliverance from Egyptian slavery, and Shavuot (Weeks), celebrating the anniversary of God's giving the Torah to Israel at Mount Sinai.

But this was the time for the Feast of Tabernacles, and Jesus's brothers were packing for the trip (of course they were His half brothers, as their father was Joseph, and Jesus was—and is—the Son of God). These guys did not believe He was the Messiah. So they taunted Him, telling Him to come along to the feast and do some miracles if He really was the Messiah. "Show yourself to the world," they said.

He told them His time had not yet come, so they should just go ahead and leave. And they did. Jesus stayed behind in Galilee. But then, after the brothers left, Jesus also went to Jerusalem for the feast, in secret, not identifying Himself. Many of the people in Jerusalem that week had heard about Jesus and were looking for Him at the feast. Some wanted to become His followers. Some were skeptics. And the Pharisees and Sadducees wanted to kill Him.

Beginning in verse 14, about midway through the week of the feast, Jesus showed up at the temple and began to teach. And His teaching blew everybody away. The text says the people "marveled." They were asking each other how this carpenter from Nazareth knew so much, having never had any formal education.

In verses 16 and 17, Jesus answered them saying, "My doctrine is not mine, but His who sent Me. If anyone wills to do His will, he shall know concerning the doctrine, whether it is from God, or whether I speak on My own authority." He was claiming to speak for God, which indeed He was. That was an extremely strong and unprecedented statement.

In verses 25 through 27, some of the people from Jerusalem who were there in the temple said, "Is this not He whom they (the religious leaders) seek to kill? But look, He speaks boldly and they say nothing to Him. Do the rulers know indeed that He is the Christ?" Some of the people there knew they were hearing God speak in these words of Jesus. But some did not.

If we are not "hearing God," it is because He knows we are not willing to do what He would tell us to do. "Hearing God" in this context means being willing to make a commitment to do what He tells us. This is walking by faith. But once we do make that commitment, we really need to follow up on it. See Proverbs 20:25: "It is a snare for a man to devote rashly something as holy, and afterward to reconsider his vows." Don't tell God you are going to do something and then not do it! That is one big takeaway for us from this passage. But wait, there's more.

The main focus for us in this study is in John 7:37–38: "On the last great day of the feast, Jesus stood and cried out, saying, 'If anyone thirsts, let him come to me and drink. He who believes in Me, as the Scripture has said, out of his heart will flow rivers of living water.'" This also took place during a service in the temple. Here Jesus was speaking to the crowd about believing in Him for salvation. But it applies to us as well, because He told them that when they believed in Him, rivers of living water would then flow from their hearts.

So what about us? A lot of people "come to Jesus." They become Christian believers. But they don't go any further. They do not read the Bible, pray, and get consistent teaching. They "come," but they don't "drink." No rivers of living water flow out of believers like that. They are just drippy Christian faucets. They are not producing anything worthwhile spiritually. In fact they are more of a nuisance than anything else.

But, God is a great "spiritual plumber." So, drippy faucet Christians, listen up! Pursue God—study, gain wisdom, humble yourselves in your trust in Christ. Be willing to find God's will in your life and commit to doing it.

Then you can go from being a useless drip to a fully flowing river of Christian witness to the world.

CHAPTER 29

Spiritual Speeding Tickets

You are driving along the tollway, heading home after a long day. You can't wait to walk in the back door, kick off your shoes, and separate yourself from the daily grind. You are cruising along at seventy-four mph. The speed limit is sixty-five. You come over the hill, and a police car is on the shoulder of the road as you zip by. You do three things in quick succession: glance at the speedometer, hit the brakes, and look in the rearview mirror to see if that police car is pulling onto the road with lights flashing.

We have all done this. And at that moment we have a clear instance of self-realization. Drivers are not supposed to speed. That is a truth. And that police car is a symbol of this truth. We all know the truth of the speed limit rule. But we tend to have a built-in sense of guilt, don't we? When we pass a police car, even if we are not speeding, we do a mental check to see if we are doing anything else illegal. And we certainly have a sense of relief when that police car does not pull onto the road behind us.

Did you find it strange in the paragraph above when I said the police car is a symbol of truth? Well, consider this. We tend to cruise through our lives without a care in the world, only to be caught in a moment of extreme spiritual awareness. We say something we shouldn't say or do something we shouldn't do. We are caught spiritually speeding. Think of Jesus as the police car. If He came back right now, would He catch you speeding on His spiritual radar?

Let's take a spiritual driving test in 1 Corinthians 6:9–10. Paul is speaking to the believers in the church at Corinth, but also to us: "Do you not know that the unrighteous will not inherit the Kingdom of God? Do not be deceived. Neither fornicators, nor idolators, nor adulterers, nor homosexuals, nor sodomites, nor thieves, nor covetous, nor drunkards, nor revilers, nor extortioners will inherit the kingdom of God."

At this point are you tempted to use that old southern expression, "He's stopped preachin' and gone to meddlin." Well, if Paul has pushed one or more of your hot buttons here, so be it. Paul was not one for what we would now call political correctness, was he?

Now, before we go any further, let me set one thing straight. This passage does *not* say that the people in all these categories are automatically going to hell. No, Paul said they are not going to "inherit the Kingdom of God." What's the difference? Well, if *anybody*, even in all these categories, believes in Jesus Christ as his/her personal Savior, then that person receives God's grace gift of salvation and will go to heaven when he/she dies. Acts 16:31 does *not* say, Believe in the Lord Jesus Christ, and you will be saved unless you are gay or a thief, etc. It just says, "Believe in the Lord Jesus Christ and you will be saved." No qualifiers. Salvation is available to *everyone* dependent only on belief in Christ.

So, what does exclusion from the kingdom of God mean in this passage? The kingdom of God refers to rewards that believers will receive in heaven. The study notes in my Bible say regarding this passage, "The Kingdom of God here seems to refer to a future time when God will rule the earth in righteousness." Matthew 6:10 and Luke 11:2 speak of this in Jesus's model prayer: "Your Kingdom come, Your will be done."

Some Bible scholars believe this will be the Millennial Kingdom, when Christ rules the earth for a thousand years. Or perhaps the kingdom of God begins with the millennium and continues on into eternity. But it does speak of resurrected believers being rewarded for having lived righteous Christian lives on earth. Let me reemphasize that it speaks of rewards not salvation. One cannot earn salvation. That is a free gift from God. But one can earn rewards in eternity for having lived righteously on earth. Practicing sin patterns such as the ones listed in our passage will cause those people to miss out on rewards in heaven if they are believers. Now, of course, if they are not believers, all bets are off. Nonbelievers are destined for eternity in hell.

Now, in this day and age, a lot of folks do not want to hear about sin, although it is featured prominently in the Bible. For instance, back when I was doing these Bible studies at WFAA-TV, the former great Green Bay Packer football player Reggie White got into really hot water when he quoted this 1 Corinthians 6 passage in a speech he was giving to the Wisconsin State Legislature. The part about homosexuals was singled out. Reggie was labeled a homophobe, among other things. All he was doing was quoting the Bible.

Out of all the categories of people who will not inherit the kingdom of God in this passage, homosexuality is the hot button in today's America. It takes me to one of my favorite stories, which I mention in a slightly different context elsewhere in this book. During then Texas governor George W. Bush's first presidential campaign, the issue of homosexuality became an "elephant in the room." Governor Bush had let it be known that he was a Christian. What would his position be on this subject? My WFAA-TV colleague Doug Fox was the reporter to ask him, "Governor, do you believe homosexuality is a sin?" Mr. Bush answered, "Doug, we are all sinners in need of redemption." I don't know if he made up that line himself, or if some speechwriter gave it to him, but it was the perfect answer.

I am certainly not comparing George W. Bush to Jesus. But that was the kind of answer Jesus always gave the Pharisees when they tried to trip him up. Mr. Bush went on to say that it was not his job to judge people. That right belongs to God. Whether you are a fan of former President Bush or not, he nailed it.

This 1 Corinthians passage names ten sins. Galatians 5:19–21 cites some of these and several more. Ephesians 5:3–5 adds to the sin list. So does Colossians 3:5–9. Now you can look all these up in your Bible if you want. But you probably don't want to do that, because all of us would be sure to find one or more of our own sins named in these passages.

Meanwhile, the good news is that even though President Bush was right, we are all sinners in need of redemption, that redemption is available to us. Romans 5:8 tells us, "God demonstrates His own love toward us, in that while we were sinners, Christ died for us." Redemption? As I have already stated, if we believe in Christ, God redeems us. We are heaven bound. But then what? Are we going to stop sinning while we are here on earth? Unfortunately not. We are still human. *But* we no longer have to be controlled by our human sin natures. Day by day, moment by moment, we need to keep thinking, *Would I be doing what I am about to do if Jesus was here in this room with me?* Well, think about this. If you are a Christian believer, Jesus actually *is* in the room with you.

If He catches you spiritually speeding, confess your sin and ask Him for the strength and guidance to keep you within the spiritual speed limit.

Jesus has already paid your fine for you—on the cross.

CHAPTER 30

True or False?

Okay, time for a quiz on forgiveness. Are the following statements true or false?

1. A person should not be forgiven unless he or she asks for it.
2. Forgiving includes minimizing the offense and the pain it caused.
3. Forgiveness includes restoring trust in a relationship.
4. You have not really forgiven until you have forgotten the offense.
5. When you see someone else hurt, it is your duty to forgive the offender.

All of these statements are false.

1. Jesus speaking in Matthew 6:14–15: "For if you forgive men their trespasses, your heavenly Father will also forgive you. But, if you do not forgive men their trespasses, neither will your Father forgive your trespasses." Jesus tells us here to be proactive in forgiveness. Don't wait until an offender asks you for forgiveness. That might never

happen. And where does that leave you? Look at the last line in this verse. I don't know about you, but I don't want to be in that position.

2. In no way does forgiveness minimize the offense or the pain it caused. Jesus was in the throes of deepest agony on the cross when He said to God the Father regarding those who put Him there, "Forgive them Father, for they do not know what they do." That is Luke 23:24. The offense was certainly not minimized in Christ's request to His Father. Neither was the pain.

3. Forgiveness does not automatically restore a relationship. I remember years ago when I was at WFAA-TV. The *ABC Evening News* was anchored by Peter Jennings. Peter had been put behind the anchor desk when he was twenty-six years old. It did not work out. Peter then spent years in the field as a foreign correspondent. He became a widely respected journalist. After those years of proving himself, ABC management put him back in the anchor chair. This time it worked. He was there until shortly before his death. The slogan ABC used for his nightly newscast was, "Trust is earned." This is a nonbiblical example, of course. And Peter did not need to be forgiven of anything. But he had to earn trust. This applies to those you forgive. Reestablishing trust precedes restoration of relationship.

4. Forget what happened? No way. This is not required in forgiveness. And that is a good thing, because it is impossible. If you *try* to forget an offense, you just dwell on it, and it entrenches itself in your mind. You may be thinking you have heard that God forgets our sins when we ask for forgiveness. We look at Isaiah 43:25, where God says, "I, even I, am He who blots out your transgressions for My own sake, and I will not remember your sins." Contextually this means that He will not hold forgiven sin against the confessed sinner. If you think about it,

you must know that this is the meaning. Being God, He can't actually forget anything! We don't forget a forgiven offense. We are just to let it go.

5. Now what if you see someone else hurt or offended by another person? You were not the one who was hurt or offended. Only the victim has the right to forgive. You can come alongside the offended party and encourage him or her. But forgiveness in such a case is not yours to give.

Why are we to forgive? I have already cited one reason in Matthew 6:15, where Jesus says, "If you do not forgive men their trespasses, neither will your Father forgive your trespasses." That's certainly reason enough. But there are others.

We must forgive, because if we do not, unforgiveness will control us. It will "eat us up." As a friend of mine once told me, it's not so much what you eat, but what eats you! I have heard Tommy Nelson, pastor of Denton Bible Church say that he has never seen a happy unforgiving person. And the Bible has more to say on this too.

Job 5:2: "For wrath kills a man." That's pretty strong! And Job 18:4: "You who tear yourself in anger, shall the earth be forsaken for you?" In other words, angry unforgiveness does not help. Then there is Ecclesiastes 7:9: "Do not hasten in your spirit to be angry, for anger rests in the bosom of fools." Ouch!

And, returning once more to Mathew 6:14–15, we must forgive because *we* are at times going to need forgiveness ourselves. Even as Christians we are still sinners.

So, *how* are we to forgive?

1. We relinquish our falsely perceived right to get even. Romans 12:19: "Vengeance is mine. I will repay, says the Lord."
2. We respond to evil with good. Luke 6:27–28: (Jesus speaking), "Love your enemies, do good to those who hate you." We are to bless those who curse us and pray for those who mistreat us.
3. Repeat these steps as many times as necessary. Remember in Matthew 18:21, when Peter asked Jesus how many times he should forgive a brother who sinned against him. Peter suggested seven times to Jesus. But Jesus told him to forgive seventy times seven. Jesus's point was not to forgive 490 times, but to *always* be ready to forgive.

And we also should be on the lookout for opportunities to rescue others from falling into the trap of unforgiveness by reminding them of God's forgiveness to us. That is actually an assignment for Christian believers. Second Corinthians 5:18 tells us, "Now all things are of God, who has reconciled us to Himself through Christ Jesus, and has given us (Christian believers) the ministry of reconciliation."

In that passage God assigned us the work of telling everyone about the peace we can have through Jesus. But where there is no forgiveness, there is no peace.

CHAPTER 31

Dear Mr. Coody,

Read Proverbs 3:1–12.

I'm a graduate of Baylor University. Excuse me, but Sic 'em Bears! All through my childhood, I always knew that I wanted to go to college at Baylor. It's hard to pinpoint why that was. I grew up in a Baptist family. Baylor is a Baptist university. We lived in Hillsboro, Texas. That's thirty miles up the highway from Waco, where Baylor is located. Okay, those are a few possibilities. But somehow there is more of a mystique to it. Suffice it to say, whatever the reason or reasons, I do bleed green and gold.

So it was that I became a fan of Baylor football early on. Texas and Texas A&M were the traditional football powerhouses in the old Southwest Conference. But for a small "church school," Baylor did have its moments in the spotlight. The 1951 season was one of them. A highlight that year was the 18–6 Baylor victory in Austin over a favored Texas Longhorns team. A BU sophomore named Jerry Coody ran for one of the touchdowns and, as I recall, got his photo in *Life* magazine the following week along with a Bible verse about jumping over obstacles. He was an outspoken Christian. And, as I mentioned, Baylor is a Baptist university.

I really identified with this guy. He was not very big. But he was an overachiever. I was the smallest kid in my classes at school. So I felt a need to overachieve myself. I had a nice collection of autographs from sports stars of the day: Joe DiMaggio, Ted Williams, and Stan Musial, to name a few. In those days you could write to athletes with autograph requests, and they would frequently respond. Well, I decided that I needed an autograph from Jerry Coody. So I wrote him a fan letter.

He got back to me right away with a nice note, handwritten in green ink on one of those buff-colored penny postcards. Yes, it was a *penny* postcard. This was a long time ago. But I can see that card clearly in my mind's eye right now, especially the note under his signature. It said, "Proverbs 3:5–6." If you think this has been a long buildup to get to those verses, you may be right. But since that day in late 1951, those have been my life verses:

Trust in the Lord with all your heart,
and lean not on your own understanding.
In all your ways acknowledge Him,
And He shall direct your paths.

Short passage. A lot going on. The book of Proverbs is a spiritual compass. If we follow the directions in these two verses, we will always know when we are moving in the direction of God's will. A compass is a valuable tool designed always to point to the magnetic North Pole. Using one as a guide, travelers can always determine exactly in what direction they are moving. In the Kingdom of God, north, in my compass analogy, is the direction to God Himself.

So how does one use a compass?

First, one has to look at it. Daily Bible study will reveal the right direction. Learning biblical principles and then following them will keep one moving on a proper course. The first two verses of chapter 3 tell us that God will take care of those who keep his commands. "My son, do not forget my law, but let your heart keep my commands; for length of days and long life and peace they will add to you."

Second, after looking at the compass, one needs to use it as the sole guide for his direction of movement. Hey, I could have said "soul" guide! God's Word is our standard for living. Verse 3 speaks to us of how to treat others. Show them mercy and truth. And keep God's commandments. Verse 4 promises a long life and peace if we behave in this manner.

Third, one has to trust the compass. That is verse 5. Put all trust in God and not one's own understanding.

Fourth, when one does that, the compass (God) *will* direct one's paths through life. Trusting God and getting all our answers from His Word, rather than the world around us, will bring blessing.

Now, once we do trust God, we must be obedient to Him. From Genesis to Revelation we find again and again that we are told to obey the Lord. We must let go of human thinking and embrace God's wisdom. Proverbs is a concentrated course on getting and using God's wisdom. Several years ago Dennis Swanberg, a good friend of mine, suggested to me that I read Proverbs once a month. There are thirty-one chapters. So I read one chapter a day. That just about fits into a month. And after I read each chapter, I write down a thought or two or three that particularly struck me. Sometimes it will be things I have noted before. But sometimes it will be something I have not latched onto in previous readings.

I highly recommend doing this. I never tire of Proverbs. I don't think you will either.

The Bible tells us at least twenty-eight times (I may have missed some), to fear the Lord. Proverbs 1:7 says, "The fear of the Lord is the beginning of knowledge (or wisdom)." What does it mean to "fear the Lord"? The study notes in my Bible say this: "The fear of the Lord includes awe for His greatness and holiness. It also means love for Him and submission to His will." Yes, initially fear of God might include fright. But that will fade and lead to a sense of wonder, commitment to worship, and a delight in getting to know Him better and better. Properly "fearing God" will make us desire to be obedient to Him and submit to His will in our lives.

Tangential to this, our spiritual compass directs us to show reverence to God. Proverbs 3:9: "Honor the Lord with your possessions and with the firstfruits of all your increase." Honoring God with our possessions means we think of Him first. Don't give God leftovers. Honoring God with our finances can be tough, because it means releasing control to Him in what to do with our money. But if we do, the next verse says that our "barns will be filled with plenty" and our vats will "overflow with new wine." He will fulfill our needs—not necessarily our wants. Only He knows our true needs.

And speaking of tough, the last part of this passage may be the hardest part for many of us. Look at Proverbs 3:11: "My son, do not despise the chastening of the Lord, nor detest His correction." When we go off course, God will discipline and correct us. We should expect it! But verse 12 tells us that He is only doing it because He loves us. It says, "For whom the Lord loves, He corrects, just as a father the son in whom He delights."

Over in the New Testament, Hebrews 12:7 speaks to this principle: "If you endure chastening, God deals with you as sons." The Greek word for chastening in this passage has to do with education. It means tutoring and training children. So when God chastens us, He is instructing, educating, training, and nurturing us. As in Proverbs 3:6. This is how He directs our paths.

Dear Mr. Coody,
Thank you giving me my life verses all those years ago. You made a significant impact on my life.
Blessings,
Troy Dungan

CHAPTER 32

Hey, Lazarus, Come Out Here!

Read John chapter 11.

Bethany is a small town just outside of Jerusalem. Actually, today it is really part of urban Jerusalem. But back when Jesus was on earth it was about three miles outside the city. Some of Jesus's best friends lived in Bethany. Most of His ministry was up north in Galilee. But whenever He came to the Jerusalem area, He liked to stay with His friends Mary, Martha, and their brother Lazarus.

John chapter 11 begins, "Now a certain man was sick, Lazarus of Bethany, the town of Mary and her sister Martha." It was their brother who had been taken ill. Verse 3 says, "Therefore the sisters sent to Him (Jesus) saying, 'Lord, behold, he whom you love is sick.'" When Jesus heard about it, He said to those who were with Him, "This sickness is not unto death, but for the glory of God, that the Son of God might be glorified through it." So He stayed two more days where He was and then said to His disciples, "Let us go to Judea again."

Now remember they were walking. And depending on exactly where they were in Galilee, they were twenty-five to fifty miles from Bethany. So it would have taken them several days to get there. And thinking back, it would also have taken several days for Mary and Martha's message to reach Jesus. Lazarus had been sick for quite a while.

There are already a few things we can learn here.

1. Christ's love leads Him to exercise care over us. We can expect Him to meet our needs—not our desires, but our needs. We don't always know what we need. He does. He would go to Bethany, in His timing, to deal with the situation.
2. Our illnesses are opportunities for God to glorify Himself, if we just trust Him.
3. God's timing is not our timing. He waited two days before leaving Galilee and heading to Bethany.
4. God will test the strength of our commitment to Him.

Mary and Martha knew that Jesus loved them and their brother Lazarus. But they were called on for a *lot* of commitment to trust at this point. We generally trust Jesus in the "little stuff," things that might even be humanly possible to do. But what about the "big stuff," things that are definitely *not* humanly possible? See Ephesians 3:20: "Now to Him who is able to do exceedingly, abundantly, above all that we ask or think, according to the power that works in us, to Him be glory in the church by Christ Jesus to all generations, forever and ever. Amen." He can do *anything*. But do we believe it?

In verse 14 Jesus tells the disciples that Lazarus is dead. But they were still going to Bethany anyway. And sure enough, when they arrived, Lazarus had been dead and buried for four days (verse 17).

The next thing we can learn here is:

5. Human perception is not God's perception. Verse 19 tells us that many of the local Jewish people (Mary, Martha, and Lazarus were Jewish) had come to console Mary and Martha. They were sure they were never going to see Lazarus again. Boy, were they in for a big surprise!
6. But this does illustrate the biblical principle that we are to "weep with those who weep" (Romans 12:15). We are to show compassion for those who are in sorrow.

In verse 21, Martha demonstrated her faith in Jesus, telling Him that if He had come sooner, she knew Lazarus would not have died. Then she says to Jesus in verse 22, "But, even now I know that whatever You ask of God, He will give you." That is strong faith. Jesus then told her that her brother would rise again. But she thought He was talking about the time when all believers will be resurrected on "the last day." She then told Jesus that she believed Him to be the Christ, the Son of the Living God.

Some of the mourners, recalling one of Jesus's earlier miracles, asked each other, "Could not this man who opened the eyes of the blind, also have kept this man from dying?" They knew Jesus could do some amazing things. But they did not have a clue that He would be able to accomplish what He was about to do. Jesus asked Mary where the tomb was located. But before she took Him there, verse 35 says, "Jesus wept." He had great compassion for these sisters in their deep sorrow.

When they arrived at the tomb, Jesus said, "Take away the stone." Martha said that if they were to do that, there would be a terrible stench since Lazarus had been dead for four days. But, they did remove the stone from the entrance to the tomb. And you know what happened next. In Verse 43, Jesus cried out in a loud voice, "Lazarus, come forth!" And Lazarus did just that—looking none the worse for wear after four days being dead, except he was hobbling as he walked because he was bound hand and foot by the grave clothes.

We should pause to note a technicality here. What Jesus did here was a resuscitation, not a resurrection. Lazarus would eventually experience physical death again. And that time he stayed dead. He will have to wait with the rest of us for resurrection when Jesus comes back again.

Remember all those folks who had come to console the sisters and mourn for Lazarus? Verses 45 and 46 tell us that when they saw Jesus bring back Lazarus from death, many of them believed in Him. But not all of them believed. Some went to report to the Pharisees. At that point the Pharisees gathered a council and began plotting to have Jesus killed.

7. When people hear the gospel, some believe and some don't. In spite of seeing Jesus perform this wondrous miracle, some were not willing to come to belief in Him. This reminds me of something a friend told me once. Drew Dickens, founder of Need Him Ministries, said, "If a person is not ready to believe in Christ, it would not help if you were Billy Graham. But if a person *is* ready to believe, even your most fumbling presentation of the gospel will be effective."

So,

8. never shrink back from telling people about your faith in Jesus, and the fact that they too can have eternal life if they believe in Him. We don't have to close the deal. That is up to God. We just need to deliver the divine sales talk. We do not need to seek approval of men or fear rejection by them. As Paul said in Romans 1:16, "For I am not ashamed of the gospel of Christ." We should not be either. We have the Good News. We just need to share it.

CHAPTER 33

Men Overboard!

First Timothy 1:18–20: "This charge I commit to you, son Timothy, according to the prophecies previously made concerning you, that by them you may wage the good warfare, having faith and a good conscience, which some, having rejected concerning the faith have suffered shipwreck, of whom are Hymenaeus and Alexander, whom I delivered to Satan that they may learn not to blaspheme."

Timothy was a disciple in Christian ministry under Paul. He was not Paul's biological son. Paul considered Timothy his spiritual son, thus the familial reference. He accompanied Paul and others on Paul's second missionary journey. On his missionary journeys, Paul would evangelize in a city and teach there for a while before moving on. On at least three occasions he left young Timothy behind to establish churches. He did this in Thessolonica, Corinth, and Ephesus. Timothy was pastoring the church at Ephesus when Paul wrote him this letter we know as 1 Timothy.

There were false teachers and troublemakers in the Ephesian church. Paul knew that Timothy needed encouraging exhortation. Thus Paul's charge to Timothy in verses 18 and 19 to "wage the good warfare, having faith and good conscience." Warfare is a pretty strong image. But it was and is appropriate. All of us Christian believers are involved in a spiritual war against evil, whether we want to be or not. We chose that duty, consciously or unconsciously, when we put our faith in Christ.

And if we don't keep ourselves aware of this fact moment by moment, day by day, our tendency is to drift away from the course God has charted for us. When a ship drifts off course, there is always the danger of a shipwreck. That is why Paul uses the shipwreck metaphor when talking about these guys Hymenaeus and Alexander. They had drifted off course big time! And they suffered a huge spiritual shipwreck. According to Paul here, they were blaspheming against Christ.

Paul said to Timothy regarding these two, "Whom I delivered to Satan, that they may learn not to blaspheme." Now, the study notes in my Bible say that this does not mean Paul sent them to hell. They were believers. You can look them up when you get to heaven. They will be there. But what Paul did do was mete out strong discipline. Using his apostolic authority, he kicked them out of the church. Paul administered this discipline on behalf of God. But be assured that God can and will discipline us personally if we drift off course in our Christian lives.

When a ship drifts off course, one of the dangers is that it will collide with another ship. When a believer drifts off course, one danger is of colliding with other Christians. That is what happened here. One Christian (or in this case two) collided with another Christian (Paul).
It was not a pretty sight.

When we come into abrasive contact with others, both parties are shipwrecked. If the other person in the clash is not a believer, our abrasive behavior causes us to "shipwreck" by neutralizing our Christian witness to the unbeliever. That is to say that in a verbal collision with an unbeliever, we set a poor example of Christian behavior. And our effectiveness as a witness is damaged or lost altogether.

If two Christians are involved in an abrasive exchange, then both are on the rocks and out of God's plan. Remember, Paul had apostolic authority. We don't. If we have a problem with another believer, Galatians 6:1-2 tells us, "Brethren, if a man is overtaken in any trespass, you who are spiritual restore such a one in a spirit of gentleness, considering yourself, lest you be tempted. Bear one another's burden and so fulfill the law of Christ."

In this Galatians passage Paul says, "considering yourselves." That means we are to take a close look at ourselves spiritually. That is tangential to 1 Thessalonians 5:21: "Test all things; hold fast to what is good. Abstain from every form of evil." Test all things. You know what that is? It is the WWJD bracelet you see some youngsters wearing. What would Jesus do? That is what we are to consider before every action we are about to undertake. The way I like to put it is, "Would I do or say this thing if Jesus were here in the room with me?" Well, the thing is that He *is* in the room with me. I just have to remember that.

Now back to these two "men overboard," Hymenaeus and Alexander. Paul removed them from the church on a temporary basis. How do we know that? He said he was delivering them to Satan so that they might learn not to blaspheme. The idea was that they *would* learn not to blaspheme. Then they could be restored to fellowship.

And how would they learn not to blaspheme? It would be by other believers coming alongside them to show them the way back to the right spiritual course. When we see believers who are bitter and angry at God or the church, our tendency is to avoid them. But look at what Paul told us to do in Galatians 6:1–2. Restore that person in gentleness. Help him with whatever burden he is bearing. The text says that in doing so, we fulfill the law of Christ.

The law of Christ here is what He called a "new commandment" in John 13:34–35: "Love one another; as I have loved you, that you also love one another. By this all will know that you are my disciples, if you have love for one another."

When we encounter a "man overboard" spiritually, we are to throw him the life preserver of Christ's love.

CHAPTER 34

God's Bar Snacks

Bar snacks are almost always salty. Why do you suppose that is? Well, salt intake leads to thirst. The more salt you take in, the more you want to drink. So consider this—Jesus Himself, during His Sermon on the Mount, instructed His followers to be God's bar snacks. And we believers today are certainly included. You think that's a stretch? Check out what He said to His followers (and us) in Matthew 5:13:

"You (believers) are the salt of the earth, but if the salt loses its flavor, how shall it be seasoned? It is then good for nothing, but to be thrown out and trampled underfoot by men." Now, this leads to two questions: What do we have that unbelievers do not have? And how do we make them want it? What we have that they don't have is hope, which in Bible language is really better translated confidence. We need to demonstrate this confidence in ways that will make unbelievers in our periphery "thirsty" for what we have.

There are many religions in the world. And people put their trust in religions because they seek deliverance from fear and darkness. But all religions depend on actions by the believer to gain favor with the god of that particular religion. And how could one ever know if he is being good enough to make the grade? This is the key to our saltiness. Christianity is *not* a religion.

Christianity is a personal relationship with the one true almighty God, through His Son, Jesus Christ. We cannot do anything for this relationship. We don't have to earn it. We can't. Our relationship with God comes as a grace gift from Him. Grace means unmerited favor. He gives us a personal relationship with Himself even though we are unworthy.

The apostle Paul explained this to the Jews in the synagogue in Athens. This teaching of the concept of God's grace was very radical. Word of what Paul had to say there spread to non-Jewish philosophers in Athens. These philosophers brought him up to a place on Mars Hill, which is near the Acropolis. The site was called the Areopagus. This was where court was held concerning questions of religion and morals. These philosophers wanted to examine Paul's teaching of the gospel.

He clearly laid out to these philosophers the message of salvation through belief in Jesus Christ. He even pointed out to them that among the idols of various religions that people worshipped in Athens, he had noticed an altar with no idol. On the altar was the inscription, TO THE UNKOWN GOD. He told these guys, "Therefore the one whom you worship without knowing, Him (Jesus) I proclaim to you."

These philosophers in Athens were searching for answers about God. Who is He? What is He like? And is it possible to have a relationship with Him? They brought Paul to the Areopagus in order to discredit him and mock him. And when he finished speaking of Christ's death and resurrection, some did indeed mock him. But, others said, "We will hear you again on this matter." Paul had made some of them thirsty for what he had.

So what about us? When we walk the Christian walk, which includes telling people what Jesus has done for us, some people will mock. But others will taste the salt and want to drink in what we are offering them. We are giving them a chance to spend eternity with Christ in heaven, rather than in eternal punishment in hell's lake of fire.

Now what if our words and actions "lose their saltiness?" Then what we say is worthless. As Matthew 13 puts it, our poor Christian testimony is, "good for nothing but to be thrown out and trampled underfoot by men." Those hearing Christ's words that day would have understood the analogy He was making. Pure salt maintains its savor. But, in these biblical times, salt was very expensive. So often it was mixed with other ingredients. When exposed to the elements, such diluted salt would leach out and become flavorless. It was then used as a coating for paths and roadways.

This should be pretty easy for us to understand too. Keep our Christian testimony pure. Don't water it down in an attempt to make it more palatable to skeptics. Tell it straight. Satan and his minions know our weaknesses, things that would neutralize our Christian testimony.
These are things such as money, power, food, drink, and sex. They are all okay in their proper places. But we must keep them in those places in our lives, lest our testimony become worthless.

Then there are things that do not have any place at all in our Christian lives, things such as gossip, slander, maligning, foul language, and dirty jokes. These things are certainly only worthy of being thrown out and trampled underfoot.

So how do we keep our Christian saltiness pure and effective? Don't just talk the talk; walk the walk. We must live out our Christian behavior for all to see. But we need a divine support system to walk the Christian walk. We must read the Bible. Meditate on it. Ask the Holy Spirit for understanding and for the wisdom to apply the Bible's teachings in our lives. We must pray for protection from any influence that would neutralize our witness. And we really need to be careful with whom we hang out. Bad company means bad influence.

And one more thing. Many people with whom you come in contact have put themselves on a "spiritually salt free" diet. They are not going to take in whatever you say to them no matter how pure your Christian witness. Don't worry about that. Do what Paul did on the Areopagus. Regarding Jesus, tell it like it is. And live like you believe it. You are God's bar snacks. Make people thirsty for Jesus.

Remember what He told the woman at the well in John 4:14: "Whoever drinks of this water (from the well) will thirst again, but whoever drinks of the water that I shall give him will never thirst. But the water I give him will become in him a fountain of water, springing up into everlasting life."

Amen to that!

CHAPTER 35

Criticism and Praise

There are proper and improper responses to both. How should we handle them? First let's deal with criticism. When was the last time somebody criticized something you did or said? What was your response? Did you respond adversarially? Did you respond defensively? Did you point an accusatory finger at someone else? Or did you thoughtfully consider the criticism and prayerfully consider the admonition? Guess which one is the proper response.

I have a friend named Dennis Swanberg who is a very talented Christian entertainer. You should check out his website for information on his appearance schedule and his DVDs and CDs. You will find him at dennisswanberg.com Years ago Dennis advised me to read the book of Proverbs once a month, one chapter a day. There are thirty-one chapters. So that works out about right. I followed his advice. I do read a chapter a day in Proverbs and make a few notes on what I have read. I never tire of its treasures. But why do I bring this up?

Proverbs is full of guidance on how to handle criticism. Other words for criticism there are rebuke, instruction, and correction. They are all basically the same thing. Let's have a look.

Proverbs 15:32 says, "He who disdains instruction despises his own soul. But he who heeds a rebuke gets understanding." Just before that, Proverbs 15:12 says, "A scoffer does not love the one who corrects him, nor will he go to the wise." A scoffer is a person who will not listen to criticism with an open mind.

Throughout Proverbs there are two kinds of people we do not want to be. One is the scoffer. The other is the sluggard. The sluggard, of course, is a lazy person. The sluggard is presented as an almost comic figure in chapter 26, verse 15: "The lazy man (or sluggard) buries his hand in the bowl; it wearies him to bring it back to his mouth." But the following verse puts the sluggard squarely in the company of the scoffer. Verse 16: "The lazy man is wiser in his own eyes than seven men who can answer sensibly."

The scoffer and the sluggard despise instruction. I encourage you to read through Proverbs on your own, looking for the words rebuke, correction, instruction, wisdom, and understanding. Don't give it the "speed reading" treatment. Don't read more than that one chapter a day. Absorb and meditate on the words. I have only given you a few examples of the proper and improper ways to handle criticism. Proverbs has many, many more.

My main faculty adviser at Baylor University was Dr. George Stokes. He gave all his students sage advice on handling criticism. He said, "Always listen to and evaluate criticism and advice. You will not always determine that the criticism or advice applies to your situation. But, at least consider it. Not every criticism is justified. But if you do not listen to it and evaluate it, you will never learn." I do believe Dr. Stokes spent time in Proverbs.

So the bottom line on criticism is that it's unavoidable. Sometimes it will come in the form of harsh words. Perhaps it will come in a form so gentle as to be almost unrecognizable. But Proverbs 15:32

tells us to just listen to it without anger. Then bring it to God in prayer, asking for discernment. If we do that, He will enable us to properly evaluate criticisms we receive.

Now remember I said that there is another side to this study. How do you properly handle praise? Improper response to praise is at least as dangerous as improper response to criticism. Who among us doesn't appreciate and enjoy a compliment? A kind word after a long day or upon completion of a particularly difficult task can be very uplifting, even inspirational. What could possibly be bad about accepting praise?

Well, unless we are extremely careful in this, receiving praise can tempt us to be prideful, boastful, and self-centered. These are things that we humans tend to be anyway. We don't need any help! Praise can actually be a negative reinforcement to us. You know what? God had that figured out. So He gave us, in the Bible, outlines for accepting praise gracefully.

Proverbs 27:2 says, "Let another man praise you, and not your own mouth; a stranger, not your own lips." Avoid self-praise. I Peter 5:6: "Therefore humble yourselves under the mighty hand of God, that He may exalt you in due time." Don't go about exalting yourself. If there is any exalting to do, let God do it. If somebody observes you walking the Christian walk and compliments you on it, this is a great opportunity to give God credit, not to pridefully take credit on your own.

In that regard, permit me a personal story. Shortly before I did this study at WFAA-TV, I had been called upon to speak at a coworker's funeral. This very beautiful young lady was only forty-three years old. Her death was caused by a malignant brain tumor. She knew that we had been praying for her at our Bible study. And she knew her time was short. So she requested that I be one of the speakers at her funeral.

This was a *big* funeral with about fifteen hundred people in attendance. Now don't call me racist. But I must say that this young lady was black, or African-American. And I am a white, or Caucasian, guy. Why do I call this is a must say? Well, over the years I have observed that black folks are much better worshipers than us white folks. White Christians tend to be rather "buttoned up" in church. Black Christians worship with zeal and enthusiastic outward expression.

As I walked onto the stage at the service, it was immediately apparent that I was the only white speaker. And the others were all ministers. I could see that I was at best a questionable fit. I had asked the Holy Spirit for help in writing what I was going to say. And He did indeed give me something. I had practiced my speech at home. But when I stood to give it, it was altogether different from my rehearsal.

About two sentences in, the minister at my left elbow said loudly, "Preach it!" And as I continued, a chorus of amens and audible expressions of approval and encouragement resounded from the audience and the stage. Well, what do you know? My delivery became much more animated. I adopted an unusually (for me) exuberant style. I became, for that ten minutes, a black preacher. Or so I thought …

Shortly after I finished, the main speaker took the podium. Wow! Hearing him speak, I was once again just a white layman that really didn't belong on that stage. During the time I was speaking, had I fallen into the sin of pride? Well, that's just possible. But, if so, I certainly got my comeuppance. I do believe that God spoke through me that day. But I was just a vessel. I needed to give Him *all* the credit. I had some confessing to do.

Now on the other side of the coin, what about giving out criticism? See 2 Timothy 2:23–25a: "But avoid foolish and ignorant disputes, knowing that they generate strife. And a servant of the Lord must not quarrel, but be gentle to all, able to teach, patient, in humility correcting those who are in opposition." If there is a need for you to criticize a brother, don't be quarrelsome. Be gentle, patient, and humble.

And finally, what about *giving* out praise or compliments? Do it! Whether the setting is spiritual or secular, people need encouragement. If God motivates you to praise someone, do it. If encouragement is yours to give, give it. But think also about offering a prayer that the compliment or praise does not lead the recipient into pride.

CHAPTER 36

The Handwriting on the Wall

This is a common expression to us, of course. When it becomes obvious to us that some unwelcome development is about to take place in our lives, we are likely to say, "I should have seen the handwriting on the wall." The term is from the Bible. It is found in chapter 5 of the Old Testament book of Daniel. And looking at the story, we can certainly see why it is associated with unpleasant developments. But we will use this story to make positive application for ourselves as Christian believers. So let's do this!

The place was Babylon. The time was around 550 BC. Belshazzar, the king of Babylon, was having a great "feast." Well, actually the language in the Hebrew of the Old Testament suggests it was more of an orgy. Well over a thousand people were there. This was a *big* party. And parties like this generally went on for several days and nights.

Well, while all these people "drank wine and praised the gods of gold and silver, bronze and iron, wood and stone" (as verse 4 tells us), a disembodied hand appeared out of nowhere and wrote something on the plaster wall in the main party room of the king's palace. When Belshazzar saw this, verse 6 tells us, "The king's countenance changed. And he became troubled in his thoughts, so that the joints of his hips were loosened and his knees knocked against each other."

I guess so. That had to be a pretty disconcerting thing to see. And even worse, as he looked at what the hand had written, he realized he did not understand what it said. So, he did what any panicked pagan king would do. Verse 7 says, "The king cried aloud to bring in the astrologers, the Chaldeans and the soothsayers." When they arrived, he told them that whoever could interpret this mysterious writing would be clothed in the royal color purple, have a gold chain put around his neck, and would be given the third-highest position of power in the kingdom.

But alas, none of these guys could read and interpret the writing. And with those perks on the line, you can bet they gave it their best shot. The queen then came into the banquet hall and suggested to Belshazzar that he send for a fellow on his royal staff named Daniel. Word around the palace was that Daniel could interpret dreams, solve riddles, and explain enigmas. So Belshazzar sent for Daniel.

Now who was Daniel? You have no doubt heard of him. He was one of a group of young men brought to Babylon from Israel as slaves many years earlier. Daniel was a teenager when he arrived in Babylon. By now he was at least eighty years old. He served several kings during all those years, and he became a valuable government executive in Babylon. All the while he remained faithful to the true God. And in doing so he gained the respect of these rulers. If you have not read the book of Daniel, you should. It is a great story of the life of a true man of God!

Now, of course, it was God who had given Daniel these gifts of interpretation. So it was no coincidence that he was brought in to look at the writing on the wall. Unfortunately for King Belshazzar, Daniel revealed the writing to say that Belshazzar had been weighed in the balance and found wanting. His life would be required of him. In spite of that bad news, the king gave Daniel the promised purple robe and gold chain and made him the third-highest ruler in the kingdom. And that was probably the last order he gave. Belshazzar was killed that very night.

Okay, now for the positive use of handwriting on the wall and its application to us. Are you ready for this? We are supposed to be God's handwriting on the wall for unbelievers. A friend of mine, Randy Marshall, is a very effective Christian speaker. He is the one who gave me this idea. But the tricky part is that we have to make sure our Christian handwriting on the walls of unbelievers is legible. They are not going to be able to call on a Daniel for interpretation.

Paul picks up on this concept in 2 Corinthians 3:2–3. He tells the Corinthian believers (and us by extension), "You are our epistle, written in our hearts, known and read by all men; clearly you are an epistle of Christ, ministered by us, written not with ink, but by the Spirit of the living God, not on tablets of stone, but on tablets of flesh, that is, of the heart." That's pretty clear. But it reminds me of an old country song that tells us pretty much the same thing. The lyrics say, "You're the only Jesus some will ever see." That should be convicting to us. Think about it. It is a true statement!

Now, our being Christian handwriting on the wall is two-pronged. First, we have to walk the Christian walk in our daily lives. People are always observing us, whether we know it or not. We need to think on that every time we are about to do or say something that would be counter to what Jesus would do or say. You have probably seen those bracelets that say WWJD. What would Jesus do? We need to imprint those words on our hearts.

But the second part of our personifying Christian handwriting on the wall is actually doing something more than not sinning. Now here is where we all feel inadequate. And for good reason—we *are* all inadequate. But, believe it or not, that is a good thing. Once again the apostle Paul speaks to us, this time in 2 Corinthians 12:10: "Therefore I take pleasure in infirmities, in reproaches, in needs, in persecutions, in distresses for Christ's sake. For when I am weak, then I am strong." There is help available for our weakness. Philippians 4:13 spells it out: "I can do all things through Christ, who strengthens me."

Let me illustrate this with a story that involves my wife, Janet. When our younger daughter was married in 1998, a dear British friend of ours who lived in North Wales came across the pond to the wedding We had known her and her husband for fifteen years at that point. The story of how we came to be friends is much too long to detail here. But, as of the moment when I am writing this, our friendship with them is well over thirty years and counting. And it is a deep friendship. We have visited each other many times, often with some or all of our children.

On this occasion in 1998, this lovely friend and Janet were chatting in our living room. The friend said to Janet that she knew our Christian faith was very important us, but it was not central to their lives. She then asked Janet, "Why do you think we are friends?" Janet said she looked up (past the ceiling) and said to God, "Please give me something!" And He did. In the discussion that followed our friend came back to her neglected Christian faith. It took her husband a while to follow. But he did. They have now long been committed Christians, actively participating in their village church in North Wales. Thank You, Lord!

Janet did just what we weak humans are to do:

1. She acknowledged her weakness to God. She did not know how to answer our friend's question.
2. So she prayed to God for strength and wisdom and the very words to say.
3. Then she stepped out in faith and went for it.

She never told me exactly what she said. She might not have even remembered later. But whatever it was, it was God-given. Janet's Christian handwriting on the wall was effective because God made it legible!

CHAPTER 37

The Eagle and the Frog

When I was a little kid, my dad told me a story about a little frog that was sitting on a lily pad in a pond, minding his own business. An eagle swooped down, grabbed the frog in his razor-sharp talons and soared skyward. As the eagle climbed higher and higher, the frog naturally experienced extreme pain, fear, and even panic. The frog was truly helpless. He looked up at the eagle and cried out to him, "I can't stand it!" The eagle looked down at the frog and said, "You'll *have* to stand it."

Life's like that sometimes, isn't it? We may be tempted to cry out, "I can't take it anymore! I can't stand it!" We can find ourselves in situations for which there is no apparent recourse or source of relief. But wait! There is a huge difference between Christian believers and frogs. Aren't you glad I told you that? Duh! But thank God for the difference. As Christians, our helplessness can be turned into blessing.

Second Corinthians 3:4–6a: "And we have such trust through Christ toward God. Not that we are sufficient of ourselves to think of anything as being from ourselves, but our sufficiency is from God, who made us sufficient as ministers of the new covenant ..."

Let's look at some of the ways our helplessness can be turned into blessing.

1. When we are forced to admit that we are helpless, we finally turn to God. In our human nature, we tend to roll along through life, mistakenly thinking we are self-sufficient. We don't seek God's guidance. Whatever happens in life, we think, "Hey, I got this. I'll figure it out."

But we need to go back to Isaiah 55:8–9: "For My thoughts are not your thoughts, nor are your ways My ways, says the Lord. For as the Heavens are higher than the earth, so are My ways higher than your ways, and My thoughts higher than your thoughts."

This passage offers a warning *and* a solution regarding our helplessness. God designed us helpless so that we would have to depend on Him. When we finally do, He says, "I have been waiting for you with blessings." Well, okay, I don't want to put words in God's mouth, but hopefully you get what I mean. God is God. We are not. The sooner we realize that, the better off we are.

2. Realizing we are helpless relieves us of the burden of trying to do the will of God in our own strength. Once again, "Duh!" We have no strength. In our self-centeredness and arrogance, we think we do. But we don't. Once a friend of mine had a plumbing issue in his house. He tried to take care of it himself. "Hey, I got this. I'll figure it out." Well, of course he eventually had to call a professional plumber. The plumber took care of the problem. And, as he was writing out his bill, he told my friend, "We love it when

you guys try to do our job. It just winds up being a bigger and more expensive fix when you do finally call us."

God is our Divine Professional Plumber. We certainly can make it a lot easier on ourselves if we just call on Him before trying to deal with our own problems. First Peter 5:6–7: "Therefore, humble yourselves under the mighty hand of God, that He may exalt you in due time, casting all your care upon Him, for He cares for you." When God says, "Hey, I got this," He really does!

3. If we are going to live our lives in God's will, our helplessness must cause us to call upon and rely upon the Holy Spirit. He is the power source Jesus left us when He went back to heaven. When we do call upon the Holy Spirit, He can even help us when we can't figure out how to pray about something. Romans 8:26: "We do not know what we should pray for as we ought, but the Spirit Himself makes intercession for us with groanings which cannot be uttered."

4. Our helplessness provides God a chance to demonstrate what great things He can do with so little—us that is.

5. Admitting our helplessness frees us to let God use us to the maximum of our potential. He will empower us for whatever He has in mind for us to do, *if* we just trust Him.

6. Admitting our helplessness and trusting in God's power enables us to experience contentment and inner peace.

7. Admitting our helplessness allows God to receive the glory for His work in and through us.

It is not easy for us to turn over the reins of our lives to God. But if we do, we will be like the man who kept hitting himself on the head with a hammer. It felt so good when he stopped.

CHAPTER 38

Don't Shoot the Wounded

Grace is treating someone in a manner that he or she does not merit or deserve. Certainly God treats us with grace. But we don't see human beings showing a lot of grace to each other in the world in which we live, do we? Even Christians tend to be very ungracious toward others. And I don't just mean to unbelievers. Christians are especially ungracious toward other Christians.

Author Phillip Yancey says that we Christians often "shoot our wounded." What does he mean by that? Well, take for instance a believer who has been found to be in some kind of sin pattern. His (or her) fellow Christians are much more likely to be interested in judging the sinner than graciously desiring to participate in that person's spiritual rehabilitation.

I found this "shooting our wounded" concept in Yancey's excellent book, *What's So Amazing About Grace?* He wrote it in the 1990s. But it is still available. Our church small group used it for a study. I highly recommend it for your reading list. It will open your eyes about how we should be manifesting God's grace in our own lives.

The members of our group experienced significant conviction in studying it.

But it is all in the Bible. There we can see that when God shows us grace, He is not just cutting some slack to His creations. He is revealing His character. It's not about us. It's about Him. Romans 5:8–9: "God demonstrates His own love toward us in that, while we were yet sinners, Christ died for us. Much more then, having now been justified by His blood, we shall be saved from wrath through Him."

"We shall be saved from wrath" if we believe in Jesus Christ. That's what it says here in Romans. But, since we are human, we are still sinners even after we have become Christians. We no longer have to let our lives be controlled by sin. But we all fall off the wagon now and then. How does God deal with that? Can believers lose their salvation due to sinning? *No*, they cannot. In John 10:28–29: Jesus speaking of His sheep (Christian believers) says, "And I give them eternal life, and they shall never perish; neither shall anyone snatch them out of My hand. My Father, who has given them to Me, is greater than all; and no one is able to snatch them out of My Father's hand." *That* is eternal security for Christian believers—signed, sealed, and delivered!

Now, about our sins, 1 John 1:9 tells us that when we sin, "If we confess our sins, He (God) is faithful and just to forgive us our sins, and to cleanse us from all unrighteousness." God doesn't hold a grudge. He is not vindictive. All we have to do is confess whatever sin we have committed to God, and He forgives it. And that next phrase, "cleanse us from all unrighteousness," means He forgives us for the sin we confessed and any other unconfessed sin in our lives.

Two things to add here:

1. God forgave all sins of all the people of the world, past, present, and future through Christ's death on the cross. So what does it mean here that when we confess sin, He forgives it? Well, when we believers sin, we take ourselves out of fellowship with God. We neutralize our witness. Forgiving us when we confess restores us to fellowship with Him, and thus restores our Christian witness.

2. But sin *does* have consequences. Even when we confess a sin, we will still face God's discipline. Some sins have stronger consequences than others. But all sins have consequences.

It is because God loves us that He metes out these consequences for sin, even sin that has been forgiven. Hebrews 12:6, which is a paraphrase of Proverbs 3:11, says, "My son, do not despise the chastening of the Lord, nor be discouraged when you are rebuked by Him. For whom the Lord loves, He chastens and scourges every son whom He receives." The Proverbs passage also says, "Just as a father the son in whom he delights." That line tells earthly fathers to follow God's example and chasten (discipline) their kids. The idea is to nudge us and our earthly kids back onto the right track— that is to say, God's plan.

And where does God put our forgiven sins? Psalm 103:12: "As far as the east is from the west, so far has He removed our transgressions from us."

And not only does God forgive us believers of our sins, He adopts us as His children. John 1:12: "But, as many as received Him (Christ), to them He gave the right to become children of God." And God also gives us citizenship in heaven. Philippians 3:20: "For our citizenship is in Heaven." He also makes us whole, complete in Christ. Colossians 2:10: "And you (believers) are complete in Him (Jesus)." And for good measure we believers are said to be, in Ephesians 1:3: "blessed with every spiritual blessing.

How about that! In God's grace toward us believers, He gives us not only forgiveness, but He adopts us as His children, gives us citizenship in heaven, completeness in Christ, and blesses us with every spiritual blessing. Now, instead of "shooting our wounded" when Christians whom we know have spiritual failures, let me give you an example of how we should behave—in grace.

Dr. Larry Poland, the founder of the Mastermedia ministry, told me a story. Mastermedia, as I pointed out in the introduction to this book, is a Christian outreach to the movers and shakers in the entertainment industry. The story concerned a top television network executive who is a Christian believer. This executive had a brother who chose not to walk with Christ. The nonbelieving brother contracted AIDS due to numerous homosexual relationships. And he became so ill that his doctors told him he was dying. How do you suppose his Christian brother responded? He visited his dying brother every day, taking him meals, offering him comfort, and showing him unconditional love.

God certainly treats us in grace. Can we not just pass that grace on to others? Consider Jesus's words in John 13:35: "By this all will know that you are My disciples, if you have love for one another."

Love includes grace.

CHAPTER 39

So Who Are the Meek?

During Jesus's Sermon on the Mount, He said (in Matthew 5:5), "Blessed are the meek, for they shall inherit the earth." So who are the meek anyway? Am I among them? Are you? What does the word meek actually mean? And what did Jesus mean when he said the meek would inherit the earth? Wow! That's a lot of questions. Now for some answers.

To begin with, Jesus was paraphrasing an Old Testament verse. Psalm 37:9 says, "For evil doers shall be cut off. But those who wait on the Lord, they shall inherit the earth." That is certainly one concept of meek. People who don't charge out on their own, but who wait for God's timing. That's part of being meek. But there is more.

The Greek word for meek that Jesus used here is *praus* (pronounced in English pray' oos). Okay, I know that Jesus was in all likelihood speaking Aramaic. But the New Testament was written originally in Greek. And I believe the Bible was divinely inspired. So the word here is *praus*, which means gentle or humble. That's good too. But it is also a word used in training horses. In that context, it means "breaking" a horse to saddle. The idea is great power under control. Now we are getting somewhere. Yes! That is what Jesus meant here by meek, great power under control.

And that should describe us as Christian believers. We have at our disposal the power of the almighty God, *if* we remain under His control. Meekness is also a synonym of humility. And it is the very opposite of arrogance. So the meek are gentle and humble. They have the power of God. But they wait upon the Lord to use it. The picture becomes clear.

So if we are meek, Jesus says we will "inherit the earth." What did He mean by that? The Greek word Jesus used for earth here is *ghay* (gay). It means region, country, earth, ground, or world. For reference the similar Hebrew word is *ehrets* (eh' rets). It means a region, a land, or the whole earth. But the root of the word means to be firm or solid.

So there are several possibilities. It could mean that meek folks will be rulers of regions or lands in the Millennium. It could just mean that they will be held in the firm grip of God. Or it could mean that they will receive a general blessing from God. But, in any case, it speaks of rewards from God. And rewards from God are desirable, whatever they are. Being meek has an eternal payoff that is worth pursuing.

The prime model for meekness is none other than Jesus Himself. During His earthly ministry, He did not assert His authority or His rights. He took on human form. He is unique in that He was and is completely human and completely God at the same time. Even in His human form He could have exercised all godly power. But He didn't. He placed Himself under the authority of God the Father, and even under the authority of human law.

Philippians 2:5–8: "Let this mind be in you which was also in Christ Jesus, who being in the form of God, did not consider it robbery to be equal with God, but made Himself of no reputation, taking the form of a bondservant and coming in the likeness of men. And being found in appearance as a man, He humbled Himself and became obedient to the point of death, even the death of the Cross." That is meekness—great power under control.

Jesus's example was countercultural. It still is. The world does not put high value on humility. Rather it recognizes high achievement, outward beauty, exceptional skills, and, of course, wealth. He exhibited none of these. He could have. But He didn't.

So how are we supposed to achieve meekness? First Peter 5:5–7 gives us instruction. "Submit yourselves to your elders. Yes, all of you be submissive to one another, and be clothed in humility, for God resists the proud, but gives grace to the humble. Therefore humble yourselves under the mighty hand of God, that He may exalt you in due time, casting all your cares upon Him, for He cares for you."

See that promise? See what will happen if we do live with humility in meekness? He (God) will exalt us in due time. Exalt means lift up. It means to bless. This is hard for us humans because that term Jesus calls meekness in Matthew 5:5 refers to "waiting on the Lord," as Psalm 37:9 tells us. We don't like to wait.

But impatience is a trap. Whatever we want, we want it now! And thus we tend to be unwilling to admit that God is in control. His timing is not our timing. But impatience is not the only trap to waiting on the Lord. There is also insecurity. We feel that if we don't get certain possessions or if certain things don't happen in our lives, we just can't function. And that is related to the trap of identifying in the wrong things. We can feel good about ourselves only if we are considered successful by the world's standards.

There are a lot of humility traps. Another one is ignorance of God's ways. We either don't consult God's Word, or if we do, we disregard it. We decide for ourselves what is right, and what is wrong. Then there is the trap of impure motives. This means being motivated by jealousy or discontent, trying to manipulate a situation in our favor. And how about impulsiveness? That is seeing what looks to be an open door in life and assuming God opened it without asking Him how to proceed. And finally there is ingratitude—a lack of thankfulness for all that God has already given us.

Humility does not come naturally to humans, even Christians. It requires an ongoing day by day, hour by hour, even minute by minute concentration on remaining in God's presence. God promised to exalt us in due time *if* we live in meekness and humility. He may choose to give us material blessings or not. There's nothing wrong with material blessings. But the greater blessing to us comes from just an increased understanding of who God is and how we are to submit ourselves to whatever He has in mind for us.

Luke 14:11: "For whoever exalts himself will be humbled. But whoever humbles himself will be exalted."

CHAPTER 40

Ratzafratz Leptarep

After considerable research, I cannot identify the source of the words in this title. But I have a picture in my mind's eye of Yosemite Sam muttering them when he was once again foiled in another cartoon battle with his nemesis, Bugs Bunny. I love the old Warner Brothers Looney Tunes cartoons. They generally involved two main characters, a protagonist and an antagonist. The protagonist in a drama is a character who is trying to accomplish some goal. The antagonist presents obstacles to the accomplishment of that goal. When the obstacles cannot be overcome, frustration results for the protagonist.

Bugs continually frustrated Sam. He also frustrated the hapless Elmer Fudd. Tweety frustrated Sylvester. The Road Runner frustrated the coyote. By the way, I read recently that a coyote can run faster than a roadrunner. Does this mean for a large part of my childhood I was living a lie?

You might be saying, what has this got to do with a Bible study? Well, I will tell you. Believe it or not, frustration is part of God's plan. Ratzafratz Leptarep! What's up with that?

Frustration can be defined as a deep and chronic state of insecurity and dissatisfaction, arising from unresolved problems. We Christian believers are not exempt from such feelings. We run into situations in life that are out of our control. *But* that is our human nature taking over our thought process. If we would stop and think a minute, we would realize that we really do not have the power to control *anything* in our lives.

Sure, we can formulate and execute plans. We can attain education and training for things, such as our careers, and function within established parameters. But problems do arise. Obstacles block our paths. And it is our natural human nature to try to fix things on our own.

The Jews of the Old Testament were always doing that. One nation or another would frequently rise up against them. And more often than not, the king of the Northern Kingdom (Israel) or the king of the Southern Kingdom (Judah) would go to a neighboring country for help rather than going to God. Often the result would be that the "helping" country would turn on them and enslave Israel or Judah. This amounted to frustration with a capital *F*. That would be Frustration. But on rare occasions, when a Jewish king went to God for guidance and deliverance, God took care of business for him. Can we please learn from this principle? God has the answers. We don't.

We go next to Romans 8:20–21, where Paul talks about how God deals with His creation (contextually mankind), "For the creation was subjected to futility, not willingly, but because of Him who subjected it in hope; because the creation itself will also be delivered from the bondage of corruption into the glorious liberty of the children of God."

What? Paul does write in a rather complex (and to me convoluted) manner. But, what he was saying here is that God subjects us humans to frustration in the hope that we will turn to Him for freedom and liberty as His children. God uses frustration as a means to teach us how to enjoy His grace. When we are out of His plan, He allows frustration to build in us until we are finally driven back to Him in prayer and total dependence.

But what happens if we don't at some point finally come around and take our frustration to God in prayer and supplication? Well, the frustrations keep on building to the point of an emotional explosion—or sometimes an emotional implosion. We either become impossible to deal with because we have explosive outbursts, or we withdraw into depression.

This takes us to the principle of "brokenness," which actually does not have to be nearly as bad as it sounds. When you finally come to a point where you realize there is no way you are going to solve a problem on your own, and admit to God that you are helpless to continue, that is brokenness—brokenness of spirit. That is the point at which you turn to God in earnest and sincere prayer, saying, "God, I am at the end of my rope. I cannot handle this. I am turning my situation over to You." Then, God will take care of business for you. That does not mean he will remove the problem at hand (although He might). It does mean He will get you through it.

I think of a situation in my WFAA-TV Bible study. A young lady in our group had a beloved dog named Idgie. Idgie was suffering not only from cancer, but also diabetes. This young lady did everything humanly possible for her pet in the way of treatments. At Bible study we all prayed alongside her as she turned the situation over to God. Idgie did die. But she said God gave her the strength and comfort to see her through this sad time.

And I had a personal experience that fits here. It also involved a dog. Our daughter was about to get married. She had a dog. This dog had a very unpleasant personality. In fact, I would say it was bordering on vicious to everybody but our daughter. The place she and her new husband were going to live did not take pets. I tried everything I could think of to place this dog. Finally a no-kill animal shelter took it. Problem solved, right? No, the dog was not there two days before it bit somebody. The dog was back with us. It was Monday. The wedding was coming up Saturday.

I clearly remember driving to work that day praying a prayer of brokenness. All that I could do was turn the situation over to God. The very next day I was contacted by an American Airlines flight attendant. A mutual friend had told her about our dog dilemma. She knew of a fifteen-hundred-acre facility in Utah that would take the dog. In fact she was taking several dogs there on a flight that she was working that week. God took care of business. The dog went to Utah and lived out the rest of its days. But I had to get to the point of brokenness and hand the problem over to God.

Now I said this concept of brokenness "actually doesn't have to be nearly as bad as it sounds." The good news is that when you have learned the brokenness principle, you can turn your frustration over to God *before* you are hopelessly flat on your face. You just have to realize that God does not want you to try to take care of your problems with cheap human effort solutions. Go to Philippians 4:19, where Paul tells us, "My God shall supply all your needs, according to His riches in glory by Christ Jesus."

This works. The Bible means what it says. You can admit your brokenness and turn your frustration over to God. Or you can keep on muttering Ratzafratz Leptarep.

Your choice …

CHAPTER 41

Get A Grip ... on Your Tongue!

This is a cautionary study. It is meant for me at least as much as for everybody else. Gossip is not a popular subject. But it is a very popular activity.

James 3:3–5: "Indeed we put bits in horses' mouths that they obey us, and we turn their whole body. Look also at ships, although they are so large and driven by fierce winds, they are turned by a very small rudder, wherever the pilot desires. Even so, the tongue is a little member and boasts great things." And verse 8: "But no man can tame the tongue. It is an unruly evil, full of deadly poison."

Most of us tend to spend a disproportionate time in idle talk about others. This may be done with or without the intention of hurting the people about whom we are talking. But not only does it hurt them, it hurts us much more. We Christian believers are certainly not exempt from the temptation to gossip. Indeed, James was speaking to believers in the above passage.

And this passage in James is not the only biblical warning against gossip. Let's look at a few more for reinforcement. In Romans 1:30, Paul refers to gossipers as, "whisperers and back biters." And he also says in that passage that gossipers are, "haters of God, violent, proud boasters, inventors of evil things."

And these "whisperers and backbiters" are also associated in verse 29 with those who practice sexual immorality, wickedness, covetousness, maliciousness, murder, strife, deceit, and evil-mindedness. Gossip, Paul says, is serious business!

Then we have 2 Timothy 3:1–3, which puts slanderers (another word for gossips), in company with lovers of themselves—boasters, proud, blasphemers, disobedient to parents, unthankful, unholy, unforgiving, without self control, brutal, despisers of good, traitors, headstrong, lovers of pleasure rather than lovers of God. And verse 5 says, "From such people, turn away." Whoa! That's strong!

And the command not to gossip made God's Top Ten list in the Old Testament. Exodus 20:16 says, "Thou shall not bear false witness against your neighbor." God wrote that in stone! Gossip does not fit into the character of who we are as God's children. You can't have pure water and poison pouring out of the same faucet!

A friend of mine sends me a "Murphy's Law" calendar every year. As you probably know, the basic tenant of "Murphy's Law" is that anything that can go wrong will go wrong. But in this calendar there is a tangential thought for every day of the year. My favorite one of these is, "If you put a spoonful of wine into a barrel of sewage, you get sewage. If you put a spoonful of sewage into a barrel of wine, you get sewage." Gossip is poison. When it spills from our lips, it reveals what is in our hearts.

First Peter 4:15 uses the word *busybody* for gossip. "But let none of you suffer as a murderer, a thief, an evil doer, or as a busybody in other people's matters." Once again gossip is placed in company with murder, theft, and general evildoing. Gossip can seem so harmless to us at times. But it is *not*.

We humans, even as Christian believers, are far from perfect. We *will* find ourselves engaged in gossip from time to time. And whenever we do falter, allowing gossip and its friends deceit and maliciousness to enter into our lives, we need to run, not walk to 1 John 1:9 and pray the twofold prayer indicated in that verse: "If we confess our sins, He (God) is faithful and just to forgive us our sins, and to cleanse us from all unrighteousness." Ask God to forgive a specific sin, and He will also wipe off the books the rest of the sins in your life at that moment, even if you have forgotten them.

Then we need to go to the words of King David in Psalm 19:14: "Let the words of my mouth and the meditation of my heart be acceptable in Your sight, O Lord, my strength and my Redeemer."

Amen.

CHAPTER 42

Living for the Moment

Read Genesis 25:21–34.

Esau is a classic example of living for the moment in self-centered, shortsighted perspective. He gave up his rightful firstborn son's share of the inheritance he was due to receive from his father Isaac. For what? A bowl of soup. And it wasn't even lobster bisque. It was just a bowl of lentils. How could he do such a thing? Esau's brother Jacob must have been a *really* good cook (and a great salesman).

The concept is instant gratification. Esau was only concerned with his immediate needs. That is human nature. We are all drawn toward instant gratification. It is very seductive. The problem with this is that it casts aside that which has eternal value. God gives us free will. He doesn't make us do the right thing. Esau exercised his free will and changed the course of his whole life over lunch.

Well, of course, we are not going to anything that stupid, are we? We humans like to think that we have substantial intellect. We have accumulated the wisdom to make educated, intelligent choices. But as followers of Jesus Christ, if we don't move our focus away from self and to Him, we are asking for trouble.

Esau is an extreme example. We are not likely to give up an inheritance for a bowl of soup. But, every day we do face choices. A right choice opens options to make more right choices. A wrong choice closes the door on the opportunity to make more right choices. Whether we like it or not, we need guidance from God on every decision we make, large or small. The great thing is that this guidance is always available to us. It comes from God through the divine Helper that Jesus sent us, the Holy Spirit.

In James 1:5, God promised us the availability of wisdom to make wise decisions: "If any of you lacks wisdom, let him ask of God, who gives to all liberally and without reproach, and it will be given to him." Seems pretty simple. Well, not exactly. Note that verse 6 says, "But let him ask in faith, with no doubting, for he who doubts is like a wave of the sea, driven and tossed by the wind." When we ask God for wisdom and guidance in making decisions, we must have faith that He can and will actually guide us to those decisions. And that includes the faith that they are God-driven decisions even when they contradict common sense and human rationale.

So what is a right decision? It is a decision or a choice that fits God's plan for our lives. It might not be the logical choice or the comfortable choice. And such a decision will probably not produce anything remotely resembling instant gratification. In this regard, Isaiah 55:8 is our signpost: "For My thoughts are not your thoughts, nor are your ways My ways, says the Lord. For as the Heavens are higher than the earth, so are My ways higher than your ways, and My thoughts than your thoughts."

And when God leads us to a decision that is way out of our comfort zone, we need to latch onto another Old Testament passage. Jeremiah 29:11–14a says, "For I know the thoughts that I think toward you, says the Lord, thoughts of peace and not of evil, to

give you a future and a hope. Then you will call upon Me and go
and pray to Me, and I will listen to you. And you will seek Me and
find Me when you search for Me with all your heart."

And, of course, there is Romans 8:28, where Paul says, "And we
know that all things work together for good to those who love
God, to those who are called according to His purpose." *All* things
work together for good to those who love God. *All* things?

A few days before I did this study at WFAA-TV, there was a
horrible accident involving a church bus. A number of children
died in that bus, which was on the way to a church camp. That
Monday morning, those Christian parents made the decision to
let their kids get on that bus. No doubt many of them had prayed
about whether it was the right decision. From a self-centered
perspective, it would be easy to say (in hindsight) that putting
those kids on that bus was a wrong decision. But, was it? God's
thoughts are not our thoughts. His ways are higher than our ways.
This bus accident did not surprise God. Nothing surprises God.

I pray that God never sends me a trial like that. I have a friend
who jokingly says, "God doesn't have to send me any big tests. He
knows He can drive me crazy with small stuff." And yet, twenty
years previous to the week of this bus accident, this friend and his
wife had lost their beautiful nineteen-year-old daughter. She was
driving home from work one afternoon when a large truck ran a
red light and broadsided her car. This Christian couple loves God.
That was "all things working together for good" for them? Well,
that is what the Scripture says.

Those kids on that bus were Christian believers. So was my friend's
daughter. They went to heaven much earlier than their families
would have preferred. But God used the bus accident through
secular TV newscasts to show the Christian witness of those kids'

Troy Dungan

parents. And, as for my friend's daughter, one of her classmates was inspired by her early death to become a Christian minister. Over the years since, he has led many people to Christ.

Now, it may seem to you at this point that I have strayed pretty far from instant gratification and self-centered perspective. But not really. Whether we are talking about Esau and Jacob or these parents that lost their children, the issue is self-centered perspective versus divine perspective. Life in the moment versus life in eternity.

We often will not understand the things that God permits. But He is always working for the greater good in whatever happens. God's thoughts—our thoughts. God's ways—our ways. When we don't understand what He is doing, we have to go back to Jeremiah 29:13. If we seek God, we will find Him, if we search for Him with all our hearts.

CHAPTER 43

What a Great Dad!

Read Luke 15:11–33.

This Bible story is generally known as, "The Prodigal Son." But I think it should be, "The Prodigal Son's Father." The father is the hero of the story. What a great dad!

Prodigal means relentlessly extravagant, luxuriant, wasteful, lavish. Yep, that certainly describes the son in this story. But what is the story really about? It is about grace. Grace is bestowing unmerited favor, giving something unearned and undeserved. *That* describes the father! And it also describes what God does for us. Romans 5:8–9: "But God demonstrates His own love toward us, in that while we were still sinners, Christ died for us. Much more then, having now been justified by His blood, we shall be saved from wrath through Him."

The Romans passage speaks of God's grace. But the grace this father showed is the human model of what we Christians are supposed to be demonstrating in our own lives. Not only did the father in this story practice grace, he was called upon to teach his other son, the "faithful" son, about grace as well. In that son's position we might have been tempted to say, "Well, I would never do what the prodigal son did." But what we would not realize in making that statement is that in our human nature, we *do* have a tendency to behave like this other son did. And denying that is just as bad. No, actually it is much worse.

Indeed, we have things to learn from all three people in this story, which, by the way, was told by Jesus Himself. So, let's get going.

This "prodigal son" had to *learn to receive grace*. What was necessary in order for him to learn this? He began by trying to make things happen in his life on his own terms, attempting to live in his own power and plan, not God's. So first he had to unlearn that. He had to reach the helpless point of *brokenness*. God must bring us to that point in our lives before we will turn our lives totally over to Him.

Now we don't have to be circling the drain of life before we get to brokenness. If we are paying attention to the teachings of the Bible, we can admit helplessness and total dependence on God way before that point. But most of the time we don't. Humans are really big on do it yourself projects. And that was the prodigal son. As Paul Anka wrote and Frank Sinatra sang, "I did it my way." Well, guess what. That is not God's way. Just try it and see how it works out for you.

The prodigal son did it his way until he got to the point of coveting the slimy food that pigs were eating. How low can you go? That was the moment the lightbulb came on over his head (as in old comic strips). He said to himself, "What's wrong with this picture? I had a good life in my father's house, with all my needs taken care of. And here I am contemplating stealing some pig food?" He thought about the fact that even his father's servants had plenty of good food. And here he was close to starvation.

Here is the pivotal point in the story. He learned *humility*. He returned to his father. How hard must that have been? He left home all full of himself with lots of money and big plans. Now he would be walking up the driveway at his dad's house in total disgrace. He had learned brokenness the hard way.

In verse 18, he pulled himself together and said, "I will arise and go to my father, and say to him, 'Father, I have sinned against Heaven and before you, and I am no longer worthy to be called your son. Make me like one of your hired servants.'" Great and appropriate speech. But he never got to give it. His dad didn't give him the chance.

Now what can we learn from the other son, the one who stayed with his father and did everything he was expected to do? Well, when that son came home and found his newly returned brother in new clothes, new sandals, a gold ring on his finger, and smoking a big cigar (Okay, I made up the part about the cigar. But I like the picture.), this brother was one unhappy camper! Verse 28 says he was angry and would not even go into the house to the feast his dad was having for the returned brother. He was not only angry, he was ungracious, ungrateful, bitter, resentful, and jealous. But, of course, that is human nature.

In verse 29 he complained to his dad that in all his years of faithful work, his dad had never even given him a young goat. But yet his dad had killed a fatted calf for the guy he called here, "this son of yours." He wouldn't even call him his brother. Well, what do you know? All of the things we are to learn from the stay-at-home brother amount to *how we are to be unlike him*.

We are not to compare ourselves to others. There is to be none of this, "Oh yeah, well at least I'm not as bad as he is!" Anger, resentment, covetousness, jealousy, putting ourselves above others by comparison … all these things *keep us from being able to receive grace.*

Finally, we get to the father. He is the one who makes this story sing. This father is the absolute model of grace and love. And not only love but *agape* love—*unconditional love.* Back in verse 12, he gave his son freedom to make his own choices, just as God gives us free will. In verse 20 he showed *compassion*, running to his son and embracing him. Compassion entails *sympathy* and *mercy.* And remember that this young guy came straight from a pigpen. He was no doubt filthy and smelly. His dad showed *love for the unlovely.* And running toward his son showed he was actively *seeking to restore* fellowship with him.

We are to let others do what they are going to do. We can make suggestions. But we can't make everybody do right. We are to have compassion on those in difficulty, even if the difficulty is self-imposed because of unwise decisions. We are to show sympathy and mercy. We are to love the unlovely. And we are to actively seek to restore broken fellowships. Those are the things we learn from the prodigal's father.

What a great dad!

PS: Note that in the third paragraph of this study I said that this father was called upon teach grace to the angry, resentful son. And the father did everything he could do to accomplish that. But Jesus never told us here that this son learned grace. That son missed the blessing of his father.

Don't miss the blessing of God's grace!

CHAPTER 44

Unequally Yoked?

Read 2 Corinthians 6:14–7:1.

The Bible must be interpreted according to the time it was written. Paul uses the analogy here of a guy plowing his field. John and Allis had not come along yet. John Deere and Allis Chalmers, that is. There were no tractors. In Bible days, animals were the "tractors." Even today in some parts of Asia and Africa folks would pick up on this analogy easily. Oxen and mules are still at work daily pulling plows. In that context, this means that in order to plow effectively, one needs to have two animals of the same species and close to the same size, age, and similar states of health pulling the plow.

Second Corinthians 6:14 says, "Do not be unequally yoked together with unbelievers." Now if you grew up going to church, no doubt you have heard this passage taught in respect to believers not marrying unbelievers. And that is certainly a valid, even obvious application. But there is more to this passage than just that. Paul gives us a much broader admonition. What Paul is saying here is more like don't even hang out with unbelievers.

But is that practical for us as Christians? I first used this passage at my weekly WFAA-TV Bible study. Let's use that setting as an example. We had a pretty good representation of believers at the station. But, certainly, not everybody with whom we worked daily was a Christian. Does this passage tell us that we are not supposed have lunch with such folks occasionally, or chat with them by the coffee machine? No, it does not. What it does tell us is that we must carefully guard ourselves against being influenced by the unbelievers in our periphery.

Paul's concern here was that the folks in the church at Corinth were developing a dangerous affection for what he calls in 2 Timothy 4:10, "this present world." In that verse, Paul laments the loss of a coworker in evangelism. This guy's name was Demas. He left Paul's team because he couldn't deal with the hardships and trials that Christians are called upon to endure. Demas gave in to worldly pleasures. He stopped ministering to unbelievers and joined them in their lifestyle of the pursuit of pleasure, which had no eternal value.

We can be around unbelievers, talk to them, and spend time with them. We just have to be careful not to "yoke" ourselves with them. Jesus Himself spent time with prostitutes and tax collectors because these were people who needed His gospel. Now I am not suggesting that we hang out with prostitutes and others of unsavory character. And I am not saying that today's tax collectors are of unsavory character. But how are such folks going to receive the gospel unless somebody gives it to them?

Indeed, we are supposed to be witnessing to these and all other unbelievers. So how can we do that without developing relationships with them that negatively influence our Christian lives? We just have to keep our spiritual antennae up at all times. We must realize that the enemy is lurking around every corner and under every rock, waiting to pounce on us to divert our paths away from God's plan.

First Peter 5:8 warns us, "Be sober, be vigilant, because your adversary the devil walks about like a roaring lion, seeking whom he may devour." We have to guard against becoming the people to whom we are supposed to be witnessing! Nobody said this would be easy. Living a life pleasing to God can be very difficult in this fallen world. As Christian believers, we are no longer slaves to sin. But because we are human, we are certainly susceptible to sin. In fact we all sin every day.

Fortunately God has given us 1 John 1:9: "If we confess our sins, He (God) is faithful and just to forgive us our sins." Confess just means to acknowledge, to agree with God that we have gotten off the path and need restoration.

So, in this "unequally yoked" passage, Paul is making a fervent plea to the Corinthian believers (and to us) to live pure and holy before God— to stay clean in a world full of sin. Now, it is tough to work in the sewer without getting at least a little sewage on you. But, you don't have to lie down and roll around in it!

Learning to develop relationships carefully and wisely is the key to staying clean in this dirty world. Read the Bible and ask the Holy Spirit for an understanding of what you read. Being involved in a church and developing relationships with other Christians there will help protect you from peer pressure that people put on you, trying to steer you off course.

We can talk to unbelievers every day, even the same ones every day. We can have unbeliever friends, as long as we make sure we are living our lives as Christian witnesses to them. Are we going to demonstrate to them that what we have is worth pursuing? Or are we going to bend over and get in that yoke with them?

CHAPTER 45

Esther and the Summit

The book of Esther in the Old Testament tells a great story. What's more, since it is in the Bible, it is divinely inspired. And it has a real application for us as Christian believers. But what about "The Summit"? We will get there, but first ...

This Bible book is the story of a beautiful young Jewish orphan girl in ancient Persia. Her Jewish name was Hadassah. Esther is the name that was given to her when she was brought into the court of the Persian king, Xerxes. Xerxes (also known as Ahasuerus) succeeded his father, Darius, on the Persian throne in 486 BC. That is the historical and geographical setting.

Xerxes's queen, whose name was Vashti, displeased the king by refusing a royal order to appear before him at a feast he was having. He was so displeased that he removed her as queen. Well, a new queen was needed. So, with Xerxes's approval, members of his staff went out to all the provinces of the kingdom to collect beautiful young virgins. From these Xerxes would select a new queen. Well, guess who was included in this group. That's right,

Hadassah, who was then given the Persian name Esther. God was really working up a backstory here!

Xerxes chose Esther to be the new queen.

Esther's father and mother died when she was a child. So she had been raised by a relative named Mordecai (probably either her uncle or cousin). Mordecai was among the Jews who had been brought to Babylon by Nebuchadnezzar years before. Babylon had since become part of the Persian Empire. The capital was now in Susa, where this story takes place.

Meanwhile, one of the higher ups in Xerxes's court was a guy named Haman. Haman had a deep dislike for the Jews. His ancestry was Amalekite. The Amalekites had been enemies of the Jews since the Jews conquered them in the land that would become Israel. He had a particular hatred for Mordecai, because Mordecai would not bow down to him as a representative of the king. Mordecai would only bow before God.

Haman became so infuriated that he hatched a plot to kill all the Jews in the kingdom. He convinced the king that the Jews were a rebellious people who would not keep the king's laws. So Xerxes approved Haman's plan and issued an order that all the Jews be killed. Mordecai found out about the plot and went to Queen Esther for help. The king and his court did not yet know that Esther was Jewish.

Mordecai asked Queen Esther to intervene with the king on behalf of the Jews. But this was really tricky. It would call for her to go to the king without being summoned. This was a capital offense even for the queen. Esther could very well lose her life if she tried it. But Mordecai told her that if she did not go to the king and request his intervention, her Jewish identity would eventually come out, and she would then be killed along with all the other Jews. Esther was between a rock and a hard place.

Mordecai told her that if she remained silent, relief and deliverance would come to the Jews from another source. Clearly Mordecai was referring to God. However, God's name is never specifically mentioned in this book. Then he said to Esther (4:14), "Yet, who knows whether you have come to the (be queen of the Persian) kingdom for such a time as this?"

Well, she did go to the king. And he did save the Jews. And not only that, Xerxes had Haman hanged. You should read this whole book. It is not very long. I won't go into the details here because the point for us is in the one phrase, "for such a time as this." We will all at least once in our lives come to a point where we really need to stand up and be counted for Jesus.

Now about "The Summit." The year was 2001, and I was emceeing an event called Summit of Christian Media Professionals, put on by the Mastermedia ministry at a place called Mohonk House in upstate New York. It was a gathering of highly successful people in the world of movies and television. There were studio and network executives, producers, and directors, as well as some actors and performers. The common bond was that they were all Christians. I don't know why Dr. Larry Poland asked me to emcee such an event. I felt like a mutt at the Westminster Kennel Club Dog Show. I didn't really belong there, but I was in great company.

The theme of this three-day event was, "For Such a Time As This." Well, you can probably see where this is going. The weekend was a challenge to those folks (and me) to stand up and be counted for Christ at risk of damage to, or even loss of, career.

It was amazing to hear story after story from these very successful people. These were stories of folks sitting in big houses in Bel Air or Beverly Hills with Ferraris and Porsches in their driveways. They had come to the realization that their lives were empty, because they didn't include Jesus. Now they were standing up for Him.

Mastermedia seeks to bring about change in the entertainment industry by bringing individual people to Christ and then encouraging them in their Christian walk in the hostile world of show business. Queen Esther's story was a great example for us that weekend. The challenge was that bad things could happen to our careers and our lives if we stood up for Jesus. But what if we didn't? God would use others, and we would miss our chance to represent our Lord and Savior. At some point we will have the opportunity to say, "This is not about me; it's about God."

In our last session at The Summit, we walked into our meeting room and saw a big wooden cross in front of the stage. It had been made by a movie prop builder. It was made of lightweight balsa wood so as to be manageable. But at over six feet in height, it was very impressive. At the foot of this cross was a basketful of little squares of red paper pierced by large nails. After Dr. Poland's final challenge to us that morning, he asked us to look inside ourselves for things we needed to nail to that cross.

After a short pause, people began to get up one by one and walk to the basket, write something on a paper and nail it to the cross. I later learned that many of these folks had written the word *fear*. All the jobs in movies and TV are really "temp" jobs. Once a project is over, then the producer, director, or actor is really unemployed until another project comes along. And standing up for Jesus could certainly be a stumbling block to finding that next job. These folks nailed that *fear* to the cross!

I took one of those sheets of nail-pierced paper and wrote on it, *my self-centered perspective.* I nailed it to the cross. After the session, we were allowed to retrieve the papers we had nailed to the cross. I brought mine home. I am looking at it now. It has been on my desk ever since that weekend in 2001. I see it every day. It serves as a continual reminder of where my perspective should be centered—not on self, but on Jesus.

Every time we have an opportunity to stand up for Him, though we know that doing so might result in rejection or even persecution, we must ask ourselves, "Who knows if we were put in this position for such a time as this?"

CHAPTER 46

What Audacity!

We Christians have the audacity to believe that God is interested in the ordinary everyday details of every one of our lives. And we have it on good authority that He is. The Bible tells us so. Oh, and I have an example.

Isaiah 40:28–31:

> 28: Have you not known? Have you not heard? The everlasting God, the Lord, the Creator of the ends of the earth, neither faints nor is weary. His understanding is unsearchable.

> 29: He gives power to the weak, and to those who have no might, He increases strength.

> 30: Even the youths shall faint and be weary, and the young men shall utterly fall.

> 31: But those who wait on the Lord shall renew their strength. They shall mount up with wings

Troy Dungan

like eagles, they shall run and not be weary, they
shall walk and not faint.

Whoa! Speaking of audacity, I start out talking about Christians
and then quote an Old Testament passage. What's the connection?
Well, stay with me here. Yes, Isaiah wrote about seven hundred
years before Jesus came to earth as a baby that night in a Bethlehem
stable. He was a prophet sent to the Jewish people. Today we'd call
him a preacher, because that's what he did—preach!

God sent prophets to the Jewish people in those days when they
had fallen away from Him and needed to be warned about the
consequences of what they were doing. At this time the Jews
resided in a split kingdom—Israel, made up of ten tribes, was the
northern kingdom. Judah, made up of the tribes of Judah and
Benjamin, was the southern kingdom. Both kingdoms had turned
away from God. In fact, at the time of Isaiah's writing, God had
already disciplined the northern kingdom by letting the Assyrians
conquer it in 722 BC.

Historically God often used pagan nations as His tool to discipline
His people, the Jews, when they turned away from Him. This
should be a cautionary realization for the United States of America
in the twenty-first century AD. The further the USA moves away
from God, the more likely He is to discipline us at the hands of a
pagan people.

So Isaiah was sent to the Kingdom of Judah to warn them about
their lack of devotion to Him. It helped for a while. But, alas, in
586 BC God allowed the people of the Kingdom of Judah to be
taken into slavery by another pagan country, Babylon.

But, Isaiah was much more than a warning prophet. He was also
a messianic prophet. His book is rich in prophecies of the coming

Messiah. George Frederick Handel used Isaiah's prophetic words in his great oratorio *The Messiah*. Isaiah may well have been the most important messianic prophet in the Old Testament. But there were others. All in all there are over three hundred such prophecies in the Old Testament. And guess what. Jesus Christ fulfilled *every one of them*. No other figure in history could claim to fulfill even a few. Isaiah told us seven hundred years in advance about Jesus!

Now this is how those encouraging words in Isaiah 40:28–31 apply to us. All those things God says He is going to give those who "wait" on Him are meant for us. Christ came to earth to give us salvation and also hope. Christ provides for us Christian believers the manifestation of the fulfillment of these promises in Isaiah.

So what about God caring about every detail of our lives? The last line of verse 28 says His understanding is unsearchable. That word in English could also be translated as inscrutable. That means beyond human understanding. He always has time to hear our prayers. He doesn't have Call Waiting. He doesn't need it. He can hear and deal with an infinite number of prayers simultaneously. Oh, and He doesn't need Caller ID either. He *knows* who you are!

Now when God hears our prayers, what does He do about them? Verses 29–31 tell us. He gives us strength in our weakest moments. He is always there for us. In fact it is in our admittedly weak and broken times that He *can* work in our lives. We have to come to depend totally on Him and stop striving for solutions to problems in our own (nonexistent) strength.

But what does Isaiah mean in verse 31: "those who wait on the Lord"? The word *wait* here does not mean inactivity. It means being engaged with God and continuing to do the things you know He wants you to do. It means making yourself available for

Him to use you. And it also means being confident that God will deliver you.

This reminds me of a guy named Larry Mullins, who used to do sports coverage on Christian radio station KCBI in Dallas. When he finished his last sportscast every morning, he'd say, "Jesus is comin' back. Y'all look busy!" Apply that to the previous paragraph here. Larry was right. That is what we are supposed to be doing. Then Larry's sign-off was, "I'll be back tomorrow, if the Lord says so too." That's profound. Keep seeking and doing God's will till we are done on earth or until He comes back. Amen.

Dr. Ron Allen has been a longtime professor at Dallas Theological Seminary. I have had the privilege of hearing him speak several times. He is one of those people who will start out on some story, and you'll think, "Where in the world is he going with this?"

For instance, in one sermon I heard Dr. Allen preach, he told us that he was an enthusiastic deer hunter. But he did not hunt with a rifle. He hunted with a bow and arrow. He told of the extensive prep for a bow hunt. He would avoid all soaps and shampoos with any hint of aroma.

He'd wear special camouflaged clothing and ultraquiet soft-soled shoes. He would pay careful attention to be upwind from where the deer would likely be. And the list goes on.

He then told of the occasion when he took his young son (maybe nine or ten years old, as I recall) on a hunt. They arrived at their location hours before sunrise and settled in to wait. The time dragged by at a snail's pace. Then as the eastern sky began to show just enough gray for discernment of forms and objects, a short distance from them a magnificent stag with a huge antler rack stepped from behind a tree and stood silhouetted against the lightening sky. Dr. Allen's son gave out an involuntary cry of excitement. And, of course, the stag bolted and disappeared from sight.

Dr. Allen turned to his son in frustration. But the son was aglow with happiness. He told his dad that ever since they settled in that morning in the predawn darkness, he had been praying to God that he would be able to see a truly magnificent deer, not to shoot it, just to see it and admire it. Dr. Allen said he asked his son, "You bothered the almighty God, the supreme ruler of the universe, with a prayer request like *that*?" The son just looked at Dr. Allen and said, "He did it, didn't He?"

This kid had the audacity to believe that God cared about every detail of his life. And he was right.

CHAPTER 47

Myth Busters

Four myths about God need to be "busted." Okay, I know that busted is not a legitimate word. It is in the dictionary only as a slang word. But it expresses a point. More correctly, this study is about correcting four misconceptions about God. But correcting misconceptions doesn't have the same impact, does it?

Nonetheless, here are the four myths:
God is uncaring.
God is inconsistent.
God is remote.
God is unpleasable. (It turns out unpleasable isn't a word either. But work with me here.)

In Matthew 6:9 and Luke 11:2, Jesus told His disciples to pray in this manner: "Our Father in Heaven ..." He tells them to call God their Father. In the Old Testament, God is referred to as Father only thirteen times. But in the New Testament, Jesus spoke of God as "our Father" thirty times. And He referred to God as His Father more than one 150 times (source answers.com). So according to Jesus, God is His Father *and* He is our Father.

What kind of Father is God?

Is He uncaring? No. He does care for each of us. Psalm 104:13: "As a father pities his children, so the Lord pities those who fear Him." What? Okay, that may seem a little abstruse. But the dictionary defines pity as having a sympathetic sorrow for one who is suffering. That's a little more understandable to our modern ears. And as we often discuss, fearing the Lord means having an awe-filled respect for Him. My Bible is a New King James, which I really love. But the New American Standard Bible translates this verse, "As a father has compassion on his children, so the Lord has compassion on those who fear Him."

First Peter 5:7 tells us to cast all our cares on Him because He cares for us. And in Matthew 6:31–32, Jesus tells His followers (including us) not to worry about what they will eat, drink, or wear, because our "Heavenly Father knows all these things."

God is *not* uncaring.

Is God inconsistent in His relationship with us? No. He is consistent. We are the ones who are inconsistent. James 1:17 says, "Every good and perfect gift is from above, and comes from The Father of Lights, with Whom there is no variation or shadow of turning." Romans 11:29 says, "For the gifts and calling of God are irrevocable." He will never go back on promises He makes to us. And Psalm 59:10 tells us, "My God of mercy shall come to meet me."

God is *not* inconsistent.

Is God remote? No. He is not some distant being. Acts 17:27 tells us that "He is not far from each one of us." He is close and never too busy for us. Psalm 145:18: "The Lord is near to all those who call upon Him." Matthew 7:11: "How much more will your Father in Heaven give good things to those who ask Him." He meets our needs.

And Psalm 34:18: "The Lord is near to those who have a broken heart, and saves such a contrite spirit." He is sympathetic over our hurts.

God is *not* remote.

Is God unpleasable? No.

Second Timothy 2:13: "If we are faithless, He remains faithful. He cannot deny Himself." We Christians will fail over and over again. Even King David, whom God called a man after His own heart, suffered repeated lapses into sin. All we have to do is get up one more time than we fall down That pleases God. He wants to give us His approval.

Galatians 3:26: "For you are all sons of God through faith in Christ Jesus." John 14:6–7: (Jesus speaking), "I am the way, the truth and the life. No one comes to the Father except through Me. If you had known Me, you would have known My Father also." If we believe in Christ, we please God.

God is *not* unpleasable.

So much for those four myths.

Now, here are some applications for us in dealing with our spouses, children, families, friends, and anybody else with whom we come in contact.

1. Be caring. Pay attention to what is going on in others' lives and seek to be of help. In matters of discipline, use

authority wisely. And temper the use of authority with mercy.

2. Be consistent. Build relationships. Set an example in those relationships with righteous behavior.

3. Be close. Spend time with spouses, children, and families. I heard Rick Warren, the pastor of Saddleback Church in California, say from the pulpit that parents today spend twenty-two hours less a week with their kids than they did in 1969. These days of two-income and single-parent families make this difficult. But maybe you have heard the expression "Quality time is the product of quantity time."

4. Be pleasable. Don't rag on your kids, your spouse, or those over whom you have authority at work

And remember, the greatest gift we can give anyone is to introduce him or her to Jesus.

CHAPTER 48

Ecclesia

I am a graduate of Baylor University. So, I never pass up a chance to say, "Sic 'em, Bears!" Okay, got that out of my system. But what does Baylor have to do with the word *ecclesia*? It is one of the words on the university seal. The whole inscription says, "Pro Ecclesia Pro Texana."
Pro means for. Texana refers to Texas, of course. But what about ecclesia?

I go to the *British Dictionary* here. *Ecclesia* is defined as:

1. (In formal church usage) a congregation.
2. The assembly of citizens in ancient Greece.

On the Baylor seal, the word refers to the church. Baylor is a Baptist institution founded in 1845 while Texas was an independent republic.

Baylor was founded to serve the church and to serve Texas.

The word origin of *ecclesia* is medieval Latin and also late Greek— *ekklesia* assembly, from *ekkletos* to call out, *kalein* to call.

So basically *ecclesia* means an assembly of people who have been called out. And definition number 1 refers to the congregation of the church. In that context one could relate it to the word *sanctify*, which means called out or set apart. So the Christian church (Baptist, Methodist, Presbyterian, other denominations, and nondenominational) is a universal or worldwide assembly of people with a common belief, who have been called out and set apart. The common belief, of course, is that Jesus Christ is the Son of God, who came to earth, took all human sin on Himself on the cross, died for our sins, and rose again that we might have eternal life. And we are called out, or set apart, to glorify Him.

Each person who believes in Jesus Christ as his/her Savior belongs to this universal church. Shortly before I wrote this study, I went to a funeral in a Lutheran Church. As part of the service, all those present recited what is called the Apostles' Creed. One of the lines in it says that as Christian believers we are part of the "catholic church." What? Lutherans part of the Catholic Church? Well, no. Notice that the word *catholic* in the Apostles' Creed is spelled with a lower-case *c*. The word *catholic* actually means universal. And Lutherans are not the only denomination to recite this creed. Many Methodists, Presbyterians, and other Protestants use it in their services as well. I am a member of a Bible Church. We could use it too. The beliefs it states are true and valid. I won't write it all out here. But if you are not familiar with it and would like to read it, you can easily find it with an online search.

So *ecclesia* refers to the worldwide Christian church. Well, we all know what a church is. But where did we get that word? The word *church* comes from the old English word *circe* (pronounced SUR see) which in turn comes from the Greek word *kiriakon* (pronounced kee ree AH kon). And that Greek word is a shortened version of *kiriakon doma*, which means the Lord's house. So when we go to church, we are going to the Lord's house.

The first time the word *church* appears in the Bible is when Jesus uses it (the Aramaic word, of course, which is *eidutha*). He used it in Matthew 16:18 when he told Peter, "On this rock I will build My church." The literal Aramaic to English translation of *eidutha* is *witness*. That tells us what we in the church are to be—witnesses for Christ.

That's what the church is. But, as the old song goes, "What's it all about, Alfie?" Well, first of all, salvation has nothing to do with attending church. Acts 16:31 tells us, "Believe in the Lord Jesus Christ and you will be saved." But when we do attend church, we show obedience, honor, and worship for God.

And He does want us to go to church. Hebrews 10:24–25 tell us that we Christians are not to forsake the assembling ourselves together. And it also says we should exhort each other to come to church. When we go to church, we have the opportunity to participate in worshiping God through song, prayer, and testimony, and by taking in the preaching of God's Word.

Taking in God's Word is extremely important, as it provides the food for our spiritual growth. Believers need to participate regularly in this divine "continuing education." As one old preacher said to a member of his church who said he already knew Jesus, "You can always know Him more." Amen to that!

And this absorbing of God's Word also equips us for the task we were assigned by Jesus just before He ascended back into heaven. It's called the Great Commission. Matthew 28:19: "Go therefore and make disciples of all nations, baptizing them in the name of the Father, the Son and the Holy Spirit." We also see these instructions to His disciples (including you and me) in Mark 16:14–18, Luke 24:36–49, and John 20:19–23. Jesus wasn't kidding around here. This is not a suggestion. It is an order from Jesus Himself!

Now there are a lot of churches. How do you find the one that is right for you? The first thing to do is make sure the basic tenant is *Who* and *What* Christ is—Only Son of God, only Savior, only way to salvation.

Then you should consider what we might call a four-step spiritual test.

1. Check the church's Doctrinal Statement. Make sure it does not compromise the inerrancy of the Bible, the Virgin Birth of Jesus, His being completely God and completely man, His substitutionary death on the cross for us, His resurrection, His power to forgive sin and provide eternal life for those who believe in Him, and the fact that He will return one day and take all His followers to heaven with Him.
2. Make sure the church offers faith enrichment. It should edify (or build up) your relationship with God through sound teaching, worship, fellowship, and encouragement.
3. Make sure the church has a heart for evangelism—an outreach to share the gospel of Jesus Christ with unbelievers. Remember the Great Commission.
4. And don't hold out for "the perfect church." Remember that if you found the perfect church and joined it, *you* would mess it up. Although you are a believer, you still sin.

CHAPTER 49

Gone to Meddlin'

The young preacher in the country church was really getting wound up in his Sunday sermon. And the congregation was getting into it. He began to speak animatedly about sin. First he addressed the evil of drinking. This brought a chorus of amens. He moved on to smoking. "Preach it, Brother" shouted a man in the back of the sanctuary. Next it was dancing. More enthusiastic nods and comments. Then the preacher started to talk about the habit of dipping snuff. An older lady in the front row turned to her companion and whispered indignantly, "Now he's stopped preachin' and gone to meddlin'."

Most Christians are not opposed to hearing the pastor preach about sin, as long as it is not one they are committing. It is our human nature not to want anybody meddling in our lives, including God. We don't like to consider the thought of disobedience to God. But that's what sin is. Disobedience wasn't the first sin. But it was a close second.

The first sin was pride. Lucifer committed that one. If God had told him, "Hey, Lucifer, don't try to be Me," Lucifer's sin would have been disobedience. But there are some things God shouldn't have to tell anybody. Lucifer's (Satan's) pride was also the first "no brainer." He should have known that he couldn't be like God. But he went for it anyway, and got himself kicked out of heaven.

Satan (we will call him by that name from now on) was not a happy camper. Now he was crawling around on the earth in the body of a snake. He was seething, looking to cause trouble. And there in the garden of Eden were Adam and Eve. Enter the second sin, disobedience.

You have heard the story, of course. But let's examine what happened. Genesis 2:16: "And the Lord commanded the man (Adam), saying, 'Of every tree of the garden you may freely eat; but of the tree of the knowledge of good and evil, you shall not eat, for in the day that you eat of it, you shall surely die.'"

Note that God apparently gave this restriction only to Adam, since He did not create the woman to be Adam's "helper, comparable to him," until later in chapter 2. So did Adam tell Eve they were not supposed to eat from that one tree? Apparently he did. Because when Satan tempted her with it, she told him that God had forbidden eating it. She knew it was prohibited.

Notice that, in God's grace, He gave them permission before restriction. Adam and the woman (Eve) had all kinds of freedom. They could do anything at all that they wanted. God gave them only one prohibition. Don't eat from that one tree. To violate that command would be the next "no brainer." So Satan was pretty limited in the way he could tempt them to disobedience. There was only that one thing God told them not to do. But that was all Satan needed.

Before we get on to Adam's and Eve's colossal blunder, here's a sidebar. The study notes in my Bible point out that Adam and Eve were apparently vegetarians. And so it seems were all other human beings until, in Genesis 9:3–5 God authorizes Noah and his family to eat meat. Even then God forbade the consumption of an animal's blood. And speaking of blood, in this Genesis 9 passage God specifically says that if a man sheds another man's blood, the offender is to be punished by the shedding of his own blood.

But back to our story. When God told Adam that the consequence of his eating of that forbidden fruit would be that he would "surely die," that was God's introduction of the concept of death to what would become the human race. If Adam and Eve had not sinned, would they have lived forever? Well, we don't know. But they did sin, and they eventually died. And from Adam all humans inherited a sin nature (Romans 5:12 tells us that). Once sin entered the world, it did not go away. When Adam committed the first human sin, he sinned for all of us. Is that fair? Well, you can take that up with God.

But indeed we—mankind (humankind if you like)—are all sinful. We *did* inherit this tendency from Adam and Eve. David backs up that concept in Psalm 51:5, when he says of himself, "Behold, I was brought forth in iniquity, and in sin my mother conceived me." And in Romans 3:10–18, which begins, "As it is written, there is none righteous, no not one," Paul goes on to paraphrase Psalm 14:1–3 and Psalm 53:1–4. The Romans and Psalms passages confirm that we are all sinners.

So *any* disobedience to God is sin. Sin is any lack of conformity to what God is and what God wants. Adam started it. But we all do it. And often, when we do sin, we want to say, like the late comedian Flip Wilson, "The devil made me do it." Nope, the devil can't take credit for our sins. He can tempt us. But he can't *make* us sin. When we sin, we do it all on our own.

Now if we can't blame our sins on the devil, how about blaming them on somebody else? Adam told God in Genesis 3:12, "The woman whom you gave to be with me, she gave me of the tree, and I ate." Nice try Adam. Nope, we can't blame our sins on anyone but ourselves. He did it. He was responsible for it.

And we can also try to deny or rationalize our sins until we develop a callousness of heart. As Jesus said in Matthew 13:15, "The hearts of these people have grown dull. Their ears are hard of hearing and their eyes have been closed." Of course He was speaking primarily to the Pharisees. But that shoe could fit us, believers who know better than to sin and do it anyway.

Not all sins are of commission. How about one of omission: not staying in God's word,—the Bible and its teachings. If we are engaging in a sinful habit pattern, we don't want to hear about it. And if we are regularly in God's word, we *will* hear about it.

Or we might say, "Nobody sees or knows about this sin that I am committing." Sorry, Psalm 94:11 says, "The Lord knows the thoughts of man, that they are futile." God sees all and knows all!

So since all of us humans are sinners, we face a big problem. There is a penalty for sin. And unfortunately that penalty is death. Romans 6:23a says, "The wages of sin is death." *But* the second part of that verse says, "but the gift of God is eternal life in Christ Jesus our Lord."

God, in His grace, has provided a way for us sinners to come to salvation and eternal life. Acts 16:31: "Believe in the Lord Jesus Christ and you will be saved." Thank You, Lord! Now, even as

Christian believers, we still sin. God has provided for that too. First John 1:9 says, "If we confess our sins, He (God) is faithful and just to forgive us our sins and cleanse us from all unrighteousness." But we are not to use that privilege as a license to sin. Paul addressed that in Romans 6:1–2: "What shall we say then? Shall we continue in sin that grace may abound? Certainly not!" The Greek word here expresses a response of shock, which can also be properly translated as, "God forbid!"

We must constantly be aware of our tendency to sin and take refuge in God's Word. Psalm 119:9–11: "Your Word I have hidden in my heart, that I might not sin against You."

And Deuteronomy 6:18: "And you shall do what is right and good in the sight of the Lord, that it may be well with you."

Modern language summary:

Obey God. Good things happen.

Disobey God. Bad things happen.

You can count on it!

CHAPTER 50

The Treasure Map

Jesus, in His Sermon on the Mount, had this to say regarding treasure in Matthew 6:19–21: "Do not lay up for yourselves treasures on earth, where moth and rust destroy and where thieves break in and steal; but lay up for yourselves treasures in heaven, where neither moth nor rust destroys and where thieves do not break in and steal. For where your treasure is there your heart will be also." That last sentence is one of two "X marks the spot" keys to our treasure map. But for many, this map is not easy to understand. Let's trace our way.

To begin with, this passage does not mean that it is wrong to save and invest money for your well-being and for the future of your family. Go to Proverbs 13:22: "A good man leaves an inheritance to his children's children. But the wealth of the sinner is stored up for the righteous." It is a matter of perspective. The second line in this verse takes us to 1 Timothy 6:10—a verse that is often misquoted. It says, "For the love of money is the root of all kinds of evil, for which some have strayed from the faith in their greediness, and pierced themselves with many sorrows."

See, it does *not* say that money is the root of all evil, as is popularly thought. Evil results from the *love* of money, or as this 1 Timothy passage says, greediness. People, yes, including Christians, can be blinded by materialism. When this occurs, they become distracted from spiritual things. The things in life that matter are eternal things, not just an insatiable desire to accumulate wealth for these few years we have on earth.

Whether we acquire money, belongings—things—by working, saving, inheritance, or receiving gifts, having the correct perspective about money and property will provide to us the second key to the treasure map. And here it is: *everything* belongs to God. We are simply managers. If we take the attitude that everything we have is "mine all mine!", we will eventually realize that whatever wealth we control is much less satisfying than we expected.

Being a good steward of what God lets us manage calls for us to provide security for ourselves and our families. But it also calls for us to remember the needs of others outside the family. Ephesians 4:28 tells us that we are to labor that we may have something to "give to him who has need." One of my favorite passages in Proverbs also addresses this point. Proverbs 3:27–28: "Do not withhold good from those to whom it is due, when it is in the power of your hand to do so. Do not say to your neighbor, go and come back and tomorrow I will give it, when you have it with you."

Here are a few other Scriptures regarding our "treasure."

Psalm 119:127: "I love Your commandments more than gold, yes than fine gold!"

Proverbs 16:16: "How much better to obtain wisdom than gold! And understanding is to be chosen rather than silver!"

Proverbs 23:4–5: "Do not overwork to be rich. Because of your own understanding, cease! Will you sct your eyes on that which is not? For riches certainly make themselves wings; they fly away like an eagle toward Heaven."

First Timothy 6:17: "Command those who are rich in this present age not to be haughty, nor to trust in uncertain riches, but in the living God, who gives us richly all things to enjoy."

The Psalm 119 passage tells us that if we love God's Word, we will realize that it is much more important than wealth. The Proverbs 16 passage tells us that if we gain wisdom and understanding, we will know the proper place of gold and silver in our lives. I love the Proverbs 23 passage. Can't you picture times when your money has flown away like an eagle? And the 1 Timothy passage says trust in God not riches.

Now when we think of things we might consider to be treasures or riches, the proper word for those things is really blessings. God is the owner of all things. When He blesses us it is our job to manage those blessings in a godly, or biblical, manner. But, of course, knowing how to do this requires reading the Bible.

Here's a story that illustrates godly, biblical management. It is called the parable of the unjust steward. It is found in Luke 16:1–13. There was guy who managed money for a rich man. He is called a steward. That is what a money manager is. One of the other people in the rich man's employ blew the whistle on this steward. He told the rich man that this steward was "wasting his goods."

This steward was in a lot of trouble. So he called a meeting of all the people who owed his boss money. He deeply discounted the debts that these people owed. And they all paid up at the discounted rate. When the steward took the proceeds to his boss, the rich man commended the steward for dealing shrewdly with the debtors.

It takes a little digging to find out what actually went on here. That is where a Bible with good study notes is a great help. At first blush it looked like the master got shorted on the payments he was due. But, if so, then why commend the steward? By the laws and customs of the time, here is the most likely scenario. The steward could see that the debtors could not afford to pay the whole amount of their debts. The steward would have been entitled to a commission on the payments he could collect. The fact that the master was happy with what he received suggests that the steward either lowered his own commissions or gave them up entirely. So the master probably got close to full payment. And the "shrewd" part is that the steward got to keep his job. In verse 10 the master commended this steward as faithful.

In the parable, the rich man represents God. The steward? Well, that should be us. The steward sacrificed his own financial gain in order to serve his master well. We are to follow this steward's example. Love God, not money. The last verse spells it out. In Verse 13 Jesus says, "No servant can serve two masters; for either he will hate the one and love the other, or else he will be loyal to the one and despise the other. You cannot serve God and mammon (money)."

There is nothing wrong with making or accumulating money. But as an old (nonbiblical but valid) saying goes, "Money, like fire, is a good servant, but a bad master."

"For wherever your treasure is, there will your heart be also."

Where your treasure is, there your heart will be also.

Everything belongs to God. We are simply managers.

X marks the spot.

CHAPTER 51

The Toughest Assignment in the Bible

Read Matthew 1:18–25.

This passage is part of the Christmas story. We hear it read every December in church because indeed it does concern the birth of Jesus Christ. But I invite you to see this story in a different perspective. It is also a story about Joseph of Nazareth. He is the guy who drew the toughest assignment in the Bible. He was a stepfather. I am a stepfather. Our kids are long since grown now. But I can tell you that raising stepchildren is far from easy.

However, Joseph's story takes on a whole new dimension. Think about this. How would you like to become stepfather to the Son of God? Well, in this passage that is just what Joseph became. And, guess what. He was up to the task. Joseph was the kind of person that we men should strive to be. He was the kind of man a woman should seek as her husband, or if she is already married, the kind of man a wife should encourage her husband to me.

Betrothed in the biblical context of Jewish culture and law of this time meant that Mary and Joseph had already made a "marriage covenant." That is to say, they were legally bound to each other, even though they had not known each other physically—not had sex. So when the text says that Mary was found to be with child, imagine Joseph's reaction when he heard that news. Now, our New Testament text does tell us that the child was of the Holy Spirit. But we have the advantage of reading this in our divinely inspired Bible some two thousand years after the fact. The only Bible that Joseph had access to was the Old Testament. There are a lot of messianic prophecies in the Old Testament. But Joseph had absolutely no idea that he would be personally involved in them. All Joseph saw here was that his fiancée was pregnant. And the two of them had not had sex. What would Dr. Phil do with this? Actually it might have been a better fit for the old Jerry Springer show.

Now several things could have happened here. In the Old Testament, an unmarried Jewish woman who became pregnant could be legally stoned to death. Technically that law was still on the books. But, the Romans were in charge in Israel now. So the Jews were not permitted to carry out death sentences. (Remember thirty odd years later that Roman official Pontius Pilate had to give Jesus over for crucifixion. Even though he tried to wash his hands of responsibility, the Crucifixion was carried out on his Roman authority.)

But Joseph did have other options. One was divorce. Even though they had not physically consummated their marriage, it was already a legal union and would require a divorce for dissolution. This could be done publicly, putting the woman to shame. Or it could be done privately, sparing the woman public humiliation. Verse 19 tells us that the latter was the path Joseph first considered. It says that he was minded to put here away secretly. Here Joseph showed that he was a righteous man. Now, *we* know that Mary had done nothing wrong. But Joseph didn't yet know that. Yet he was willing to forgive Mary. He was a forgiving man. And remember that verse 19 says he was "minded" to put her away secretly. That means that he gave the matter considerable thought. Joseph was a thoughtful and considerate man.

The story takes a really big turn in verses 20 and 21. An angel came to Joseph in a dream and told him about Mary's conception being of the Holy Spirit. And Joseph was spiritually stable enough to accept this angelic explanation. It brought him peace in this very difficult situation. Joseph was a spiritually stable and peaceful man. His determination to follow the angel's instructions and keep Mary as his wife showed he was not afraid to suffer shame. And he would get plenty of that. Most people would not know of the immaculate conception. Or even if they heard about it, would not believe it. Joseph here showed that he was a fearless and humble man.

In verse 21 the angel gave Joseph another instruction. The angel said, "Mary will bring forth a Son and you (Joseph) will call His name Jesus, for He will save people from their sins." Joseph didn't say, "Well, okay, I will stay married to Mary, but I am going to name the boy Joe Jr. That way maybe I can convince the neighbors that I am actually his father." Nope, the text says that Joseph did as the angel told him. Joseph was a responsible man.

Then in verses 24 and 25: "Joseph, being aroused from sleep, did as the angel commanded him. He took to him his wife (Mary) and did not (physically) know her until she had brought forth her firstborn son. And he (Joseph) called His name Jesus." He did as the angel instructed him. Joseph was a man obedient to authority. And this also illustrates that he was a patient and self-controlled man.

Side note here: The text says that Joseph did not know Mary physically until after she brought forth her firstborn son. The language here clearly indicates that Mary was only a virgin until after the birth of Jesus. And "firstborn" son indicates that she would have other children. I take these two things directly from the study notes in my NKJV Thomas Nelson Study Bible. Scripture does tell us that Jesus had brothers. Of course, they would have been born of the union of Mary and Joseph. Joseph could not have had children from a relationship prior to his marriage to Mary, because under Jewish law Jesus would not have been heir to the throne of David (as the first son of Joseph). Joseph was in the Davidic line, being descended from David through Solomon. Mary was also descended from David, through Nathan.

Disclaimer to side note: I once taught this study to a group that included some Catholic believers. They took this issue up with me after the study. These folks said they believed that Mary was a virgin all her life and had no children other than Jesus. We agreed to disagree on both issues.

Now I mentioned above that both Joseph and Mary were in the line of David, which is the messianic line. It is important that both were in this line. Although Joseph was not Jesus's biological father, under Jewish law he was the legal father of Jesus, thus the validity of the messianic line through Joseph—the legal connection. Mary was Jesus's biological mother, thus the validity of the physical bloodline requirement was established. God thinks of everything!

And to carry this one step further, Jesus had to be Joseph's oldest son in order to be heir to the throne of David. The law of primogeniture was part of the Jewish culture. Only an oldest son would inherit any kind of title. But what else had to happen in order for Jesus to claim heirship to that throne? Being an heir means you inherit something. *But* you only can inherit something when somebody dies. So Joseph knew from the get-go when the angel spoke to him in the dream that he would have to die before

Jesus's ministry on earth could come to fruition. The last time Joseph is mentioned in the Bible is when Jesus was about twelve years old. Joseph was a self-sacrificing man.

So what kind of man was Joseph? He was just and righteous. He was forgiving. He was thoughtful and considerate. He was spiritually stable and had inner peace. He was fearless and humble. He was responsible and obedient to authority. He was patient and self-controlled. And he was self-sacrificing. He was the kind of man that God could use. And God did use him—big time.

Looking at our own lives, we need to ask ourselves, "How do we stack up against Joseph's example?"

CHAPTER 52

Okay, Here's What I Experienced

This study is about giving people our Christian testimony. But I didn't use the word *testimony* in the title because it sounds a little too "churchy." It is a perfectly good word, but using it when you start to talk about Jesus might just scare off some folks. The other "churchy" word in this context is *witness*. That word even scares us Christians! When the preacher looks us in the eye and says we need to get out and share our witness, we tend to think, "I can't do that. I don't know how." Actually you can, and you do know how. Let me try to clear this up.

Witness and testimony are actually courtroom words. When you testify (give testimony) as a witness in a trial, what are you really doing? You are telling the story of your personal experience in relation to the trial in court. You are saying, "Okay, here's what I experienced." If you are called as a witness in a court case, that is all you have to do, just tell the court what you personally experienced.

The reason we have courtroom trials is generally that two or more parties have disagreement over something that has happened.

226

People can make different assumptions about the case at hand. They can have different interpretations as to how the law applies to the case. Lawyers can debate these kinds of things ad infinitum, ad nauseum. *But* our personal stories are not up for debate. If we personally see something or experience something, nobody has the right to tell us that we didn't. It is *our* story. Famous Christian author and speaker Josh McDowell has a really neat way of answering people when they ask him how he knows he is saved. Josh says, "I was there when it happened."

I would like to take us to a Bible story in Acts 8:26–39. I am going to summarize it here. But I encourage you to read it on your own. When the story begins, a believer named Philip is walking along the road from Jerusalem to Gaza. This was the main road people took to get from Jerusalem to Africa. Philip was a believer in Jesus. I don't call him Christian because that word was not yet in general usage. But that is what he was. He was just walking along, minding his own business, when God produced a divine appointment for him.

Philip saw this guy alongside the road, sitting in a chariot, reading something. As it turns out, he was reading in Isaiah. Philip strolled over to him, observed what he was reading and asked the guy if he understood it. The guy said, "How can I unless someone guides me?" We should all be on the lookout for divine appointments and be ready for them. Philip recognized this one, and he was ready for it.

The guy asked Philip to come up in the chariot with him. There Philip explained to him the messianic prophecy he was reading in Isaiah and told him that the Messiah had indeed come in the person of Jesus Christ. The guy immediately became a believer. There was water nearby, and at this new believer's request, Philip baptized him. And, by the way, this guy with the chariot was not just your average everyday traveler. He was the treasurer of the government of the country of Ethiopia!

Now if you read this passage, you will note that the text calls him a eunuch, which is the term used for a male who has been emasculated.
But the study notes in my Bible indicate that was not likely the meaning of that word in this context. In the first century AD, the word *eunuch* had become a government title given to important political or military officials. This guy was high up in the government power structure in Egypt.

Why did I use this story in a study about personal testimony or witness? Well, there was this fellow named Irenaeus, who is historically identified as an "early church father." He was a pastor and church leader in the second century AD (about 130–200) who did a lot of writing. Irenaeus's writings were extrabiblical, but scholars consider them historically accurate.

Irenaeus wrote about this Ethiopian eunuch. According to Irenaeus, the guy returned home to Ethiopia after his life-changing encounter with Philip and became a missionary for Christ among his own people. He went home and told everybody about his own personal experience. This is a great example of giving one's personal testimony. Nobody could discredit it. He was "there when it happened."

But all our testimonies are unique. Each will have a different focus. Some are dramatic, as with this Ethiopian. Some are not. Take mine, for instance.

I became a Christian when I was a little kid. I was probably seven or eight. I grew up in a small Texas town where almost everybody was a Christian, including my family. I came to a gradual understanding of who Jesus is and my need for Him. I was baptized when I was eight or nine. But I had truly been a Christian believer for a long time before that. But wait. That's not the focus of my testimony. That story is in the introduction to this book. It took me until I was sixty-two years old to start telling people about my personal Christian belief. It's never too late to start, of course. But it s never too early either!

I once read a devotional by Dr. Charles Stanley that suggested that it would be a good idea during our quiet times with God every day to write some notes on our own personal faith story. Then, when I was an elder in our church, the chairman of the Elder Board actually made that an assignment. And I am glad he did. It prompted me to work out a brief scripturally based explanation of why I believe in Christ and why I would love for others to believe in Him. I give it to people whom I care about—people whom I suspect are not believers and people whom I know are not believers. It is only one page. It does not need to be long.

When I give this little "love note" to people, I always remind myself that I need to remember day by day, and even moment by moment, my self-accountability in doing so. I have to ask myself, does my character, language, and behavior testify to those around me of God's power and grace? Or is there something in me that contradicts the message of Christ?

When one gives testimony in court, one is asked to raise his/her hand and swear that his/her testimony is the truth and nothing but the truth. Many courts also still add to that, "so help me God." We can give our Christian testimony. We even already know how to do it. We are just saying, "Okay, here's what I experienced with Jesus Christ." But we must remember to remain true to that testimony in our daily lives.

CHAPTER 53

Lagniappe

Lagniappe (pronounced lan -yap'): Something extra, given for good measure, an unexpected gift. American French or "Cajun." First known use in 1844.

Here is my lagniappe to you for reading these Bible studies. This would normally be called an epilogue. But I prefer lagniappe because it is my gift to you. I pray that you will use it well.

In 2009, when I was an elder at Dallas Bible Church, the chairman of the Elder Board gave all of us on that board (including himself) an assignment. We were each to write a brief statement of our personal Christian testimony to use in witnessing to people. This is what I was talking about in the last study in this collection, "Okay, Here's What I Experienced." I wrap up this book with the complete text of what I wrote for that assignment.

This is the "love note" I give to people about whom I care, who are not Christian believers, or whose Christian faith is not evident.

Please read it all the way through. At the end I have a couple of closing remarks for you.

***

I grew up in a small Texas town where almost everybody was a Christian. My parents were Christians. All my family members were Christians. My friends were Christians. And I became a believer in the Lord Jesus Christ when I was just a little kid. I walked down the aisle in the First Baptist Church of Hillsboro, Texas, to make my public profession of faith when I was maybe eight or nine. But I had already been a believer for some time before I did that.

All those years since then, I have been secure in the knowledge that when I die I will spend eternity in heaven with Jesus and all the other folks that followed Him in faith while they were here on earth. Now such surety of faith needs to be based on something rock solid. That is the Bible. I believe that the Bible, in its entirety, is the inerrant and inspired Word of God. Why do I believe this? And why do I believe that the Bible is the sole authority by which I should live?

Well, the Old Testament of the Bible is a well-documented and verifiable history of the Jewish people. But it also has over three hundred prophecies about a coming Messiah. Messiah means deliverer. *All* of these prophecies were fulfilled by Jesus Christ. Nobody else in history fulfills even a few of them.

The New Testament of the Bible then demonstrates Jesus's identity as the Messiah by showing His fulfillment of all those Old Testament prophecies. The New Testament also records in several passages that while Jesus was on earth, He identified Himself as the Son of God. He also said in John 14:6, "I am the way, the truth and the life. No man comes to the Father except through Me." Why is that so important? It is important because Romans 3:23 tells us that all humans sin and fall short of the glory of God. And Romans 6:23 goes on to say that the wages of sin is death. As sinners, we must find a way to have a relationship with God to avoid eternal death and punishment in hell.

Fortunately God provided a way. John 3:16 says, "God so loved the world that He gave His only begotten Son, that whoever believes in Him shall not perish, but have eternal life." And Romans 5:8–9 tell us, "God demonstrates His own love for us in that while we were still sinners, Christ died for us. Much more then, having now been justified by His blood, we will be saved from wrath through Him." Yes, the Bible promises us salvation and eternal life through Jesus Christ and only through Jesus Christ. And that's what I believe. In fact I am staking my eternal future on it!

But what about you? Acts 16:31 says, "Believe in the Lord Jesus Christ and you will be saved." It's that simple. Because I care about you, I strongly urge you to consider Jesus. But, let me also say this. This is America. You are free to believe in whatever you want, or to believe in nothing at all. Even if you never believe in Jesus, I will still care about you and be your friend, if you will have me as a friend. But I truly would like to continue our friendship in heaven. And there is only one way that is going to happen.

Life is short. Eternity is long. Hell is hot. Jesus is the only answer!

***

When I was doing these Bible studies at WFAA-TV, I discovered that my primary spiritual gift is encouragement. I learned that from the folks who regularly attended the studies. And I want to end this book by encouraging you. If you are not yet a Christian believer and somehow have made it all the way through this book anyway, my testimony is for you. I encourage you to consider Jesus. He *is* the only way.

And if you are already a Christian believer, I encourage you to take my testimony here and plug in your own story where mine is. Then use the Scriptures I provided. It will then become your, "Okay, Here's What I Experienced" testimony and witness. Give it to people about whom you care. And then pray for them.

God bless,

Troy Dungan

For inquires regarding speaking engagements, book signings, or other business proposals for Troy Dungan, contact:

Sooze Johnson
The Agency Dallas
sooze@theagencydallas.com
Office phone: 214-485-7200

CPSIA information can be obtained at www.ICGtesting.com
Printed in the USA
LVOW11s0843170416

484012LV00001B/180/P